Concussions and Our Kids

Concussions and Our Kids

AMERICA'S LEADING EXPERT ON
HOW TO PROTECT YOUNG ATHLETES
AND KEEP SPORTS SAFE

ROBERT CANTU, M.D.
and Mark Hyman

Houghton Mifflin Harcourt
BOSTON • NEW YORK
2012

For information about permission to reproduce selections from this book,
write to Permissions, Houghton Mifflin Harcourt Publishing Company,
215 Park Avenue South, New York, New York 10003.

www.hmhbooks.com

Library of Congress Cataloging-in-Publication Data
Cantu, Robert C.
Concussions and our kids : America's leading expert on how to protect young athletes
and keep sports safe / Robert Cantu and Mark Hyman.
p. ; cm.
Includes index.
ISBN 978-0-547-77394-0
I. Hyman, Mark. II. Title.
[DNLM: 1. Brain Concussion. 2. Adolescent. 3. Athletes. 4. Athletic Injuries —
prevention & control. 5. Child. WL 354]
617.1′027083 — dc23   2012014029

Book design by Brian Moore
All illustrations by Greg Maxson Illustration

Printed in the United States of America
DOC 10 9 8 7 6 5 4 3 2 1

PHOTO CREDITS: page 38, Joel Weiss; page 70, photo by Susan Morrow, SwickPix, LLC; page 77, Susan Osmers; page 79, Kellie Merner; page 81, Dave Caron; page 91, Dr. Robert Cantu; page 93, The BU Center for the Study of Traumatic Encephalopathy; page 116, Kathy Gallagher; page 128, Scott Clarke/ESPN; page 131, Daryl Brown Photography; page 134, Louis Walker III; page 137, Jill Lohrfink; page 140, photo by Matt McKeon; page 151, Deborah Chapman.

Contents

Concussions and Our Kids

1

What Is a Concussion?

We need to do something now, this minute. Too many kids are at risk.
— Dr. Ann McKee (*Time*)

We still have this culture where it's hard to convince people that a concussion is a very serious brain injury.
— Dawn Comstock, principal investigator, Center for Injury Research and Policy, The Research Institute, Nationwide Children's Hospital, Ohio State University (*Time*)

I N THE LATE 1950S, I was a student at Cal-Berkeley and a member of Cal's baseball team. We were playing Stanford one afternoon, and I came to bat. This was the dark ages before batters wore helmets with ear flaps. Our protection — if you can call it that — was a flimsy liner inside our felt caps.

A pitch came inside and tight, and I didn't react as quickly as I needed to. The ball caught me flush on the side of the head. The cap and the hard liner were just about worthless. The force of the blow stunned me, and I wobbled a bit as I made my way down the line to first base. This didn't seem to bother anyone as much as the blood trickling from my ear. It wasn't really coming from my ear — the force of the pitch had shattered the cap liner, which sliced into my scalp.

The coaches didn't know that, of course. They took one look at me and thought, "My God, Cantu has a skull fracture! Get him to the hospital!"

In those days, it wouldn't have occurred to anyone in either dugout that I might have had a concussion. Even at the hospital it wasn't diagnosed. It's only looking back with years of experience in this field that I can say — based on my symptoms, which included not knowing where I was for a while, lightheadedness, and a violent headache — that I certainly had a concussion.

We've come a long way since those unenlightened times. Now head trauma in sports is a topic that leads nightly newscasts and is debated at every level of amateur and professional sports. I knew that concussions had become something of a national obsession when Jerry Seinfeld built an entire monologue around the question "Why did we invent the helmet?" Normally, there isn't a lot of humor associated with head trauma of any kind, but Seinfeld's take is amusing. First, he says, we invented sports, the main feature of which is slamming our heads into each other over and over. Then, "We chose not to avoid these activities but to make little plastic hats so we could continue our head-cracking lifestyles."

A Concussion Is . . .

The word derives from the Latin *concutere* for "to shake violently." Concussions are just that — a shaking of the brain inside the skull that changes the alertness of the injured person. That change can be relatively mild. (She is slightly dazed.) It can be profound. (She falls unconscious.) Both fall within the definition.

According to the Centers for Disease Control and Prevention, almost four million sports- and recreation-related concussions are recognized every year, with many times that number occurring but going unrecognized. For young people ages fifteen to twenty-four years, sports are the second leading cause of traumatic brain injury behind only motor vehicle crashes. According to research by the *New York Times,* at least fifty youth football players (high school or younger) from twenty different states have died or sustained serious head injuries on the field since 1997. One study estimates that the likelihood of an athlete in a contact sport experiencing a recognized concussion is as high as 20 percent each season. In my office, there is a very discernible cycle in the number of concussion patients. In the fall (football season) and winter (ice hockey) the numbers go up, sometimes exceeding fifteen new young athletes with a concussion per week. In the spring and summer, they slide back down.

How They Happen

Concussions happen to all types of athletes — young and old, boys and girls, and in every conceivable sport. In a typical year, I see hundreds of children and adolescents in my office. We see more than athletes, of course. Some patients have suffered concussions in traffic accidents, mishaps around the house (they walked into a door), or a slip and fall in the grocery store.

In a chapter later in this book, I offer observations about concussions in "non-collision" sports such as volleyball and tennis that parents — for good reason — do not think of as posing a great risk of concussion. However, there is risk in every sport. I would have to think a long time before naming one that has not sent a single patient to our office at Emerson Hospital in Concord, Massachusetts.

Many patients get well over two to three weeks, pretty much as expected. Other cases take unexpected turns. Mario was an eleven-year-old kid making one of those typical recoveries. After his concussion, he had a number of symptoms. We held him back from sports, gym, and physical activity. He was also under restrictions regarding his schoolwork. Just as he was about ready to resume normal activity, Mario hit his head on a bedpost and suffered another concussion. The process started all over again. I can't count the number of stories like that. Unfortunately, they happen a lot.

Concussions in sports occur when an athlete is slammed and makes sudden and forceful contact. That contact can be with the ground, court, or pool deck. It also can be with a batted ball, a thrown ball, a kicked ball, a goalpost (football), the boards (hockey), the scorer's table (basketball), and of course another player. Dylan Mello, a high school soccer and ice hockey player from Rhode

Island, suffered a severe concussion in a collision with a player who smashed him with the plaster cast on his arm.

Concussions can and frequently do occur without any contact with the head. Rather, the player's body receives a jolt that causes his shoulders and head to change speed or direction violently. It's the whiplash effect. Inside the skull, the brain shifts in the cerebrospinal fluid and bangs against the inside of the skull. Even falling from five or six feet and landing upright, if it's unexpected, and therefore jarring, can send a shock through the spine and shake the head with a force that may cause a concussion. Concussions that are the most damaging to the brain tend to be the ones that involve a direct blow to the head, however. When you're struck in the head, the forces generated are about fifty times greater than being struck in another part of the body.

With such a blow, the brain pushes forward until it crashes into the skull, reverses, and bumps against the back of the skull.

Two Forces

Concussions are caused by two types of accelerations. In this book we'll refer to them not as accelerations but as forces. It's a shorthand that might make an invisible and somewhat obtuse idea easier to think about. (There is a difference between the two, as noted in Newton's law: force equals acceleration multiplied by mass.)

The first of the two forces is linear. It's akin to the straight-on force of a car smashing into a tree. At the moment of impact, the driver's head snaps violently. The collisions cause injury, of course. That damage is worse than it would otherwise be because the inside of the skull is rough, not smooth. Contact between the brain tissue and the bony surface can be irritating, sometimes bruising or even tearing brain tissue.

The second type of force is rotational. Think of a football player running from sideline to sideline and a head-hunting defensive player appearing out of nowhere to make a crunching tackle from the side. The force of the collision violently whips the ball carrier's

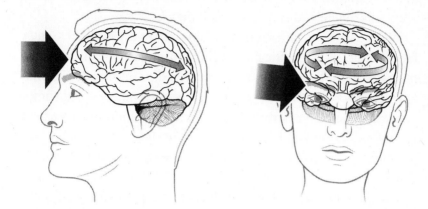

Linear Acceleration *(left)*: A straight-line acceleration that snaps the head. An impact to the front of the head moves the brain backward, making contact with the back of the skull, then forward, resulting in a second impact with the front of the skull. A side impact results in side-to-side movement of the brain. **Rotational Acceleration** *(right)*: This acceleration is more damaging to the brain than a linear acceleration. It is caused by an off-center or tangential hit that causes the brain to rotate or spin within the skull.

head to one side. If it's jolting enough, the brain comes into contact with the skull. The cerebrospinal fluid in which the brain floats protects the brain and dampens the impact. However, if the force is large enough, an injury occurs. Driven into the skull by rotational forces, the brain can stretch and shear. Blood vessels and brain tissue are exposed to trauma and may tear.

The effects of rotational forces can be much worse than those from linear forces. Concern about them caused the NFL to outlaw blind-side or "defenseless player" helmet-to-helmet hits. On virtually every hit to the head, both the linear and rotational accelerations are present. Among researchers and other experts, it's believed that rotational forces are more injurious.

Changes to the brain's structure — tears and other injuries — are difficult to see. They're often invisible on head CT scans and routine magnetic resonance imaging (MRI), the imaging tests most relied on. For that reason, there are misconceptions about the damage that occurs to the brain from a concussion. Through the years, even medical professionals have questioned whether the structure of the brain was different after a concussion than before.

We know now that in some cases, the answer is yes. At the Center for the Study of Traumatic Encephalopathy at Boston University, the brains of more than one hundred deceased professional and amateur athletes have been studied. Several of these athletes died within days of a concussion. Several of their deaths were suicides. As one of the cofounders of CSTE, I'm familiar with these cases. The brains I am referring to were examined by my colleague, Dr. Ann McKee, a world-renowned neuropathologist.

The patients had widespread diffuse axonal swelling and other abnormalities that would have been missed if they had been tested when they were living. Some of the changes were limited to one region of the brain. In other cases, changes happened over several areas from the cortex and brain stem down to the spinal cord. All the injuries were microscopic. But they were and are real.

Metabolic Changes

Concussions also trigger a complicated chain of chemical and metabolic reactions, which are known as the neurometabolic cascade of concussion. This process confuses the brain, throwing off its ability to regulate, to transmit signals, and to send messages that control how we think and what we remember.

From being pushed and pulled violently, the brain goes into an overactive state, a state of hyperalertness, releasing chemicals called neurotransmitters. These are the chemicals needed for one cell to communicate with the next and the next. In this situation, the cells begin communicating in a disorderly way, blasting out impulses to all cells at the same time so that the system becomes overloaded. At this point the brain loses its ability to regulate certain chemical balances. Potassium ions, which are typically contained within brain cells, flood out. Calcium ions, which are on the outside, rush inside the cells. The brain's chemical batting order is turned upside down, and returning things to normal is a very difficult process. To

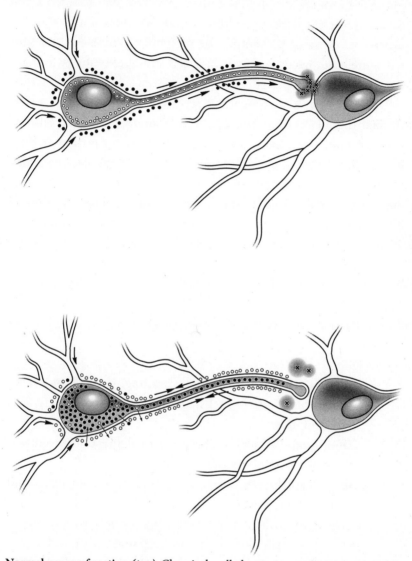

Normal neuron function *(top)*: Chemicals called neurotransmitters move among nerve cells in the brain, sending messages. For the process to work efficiently, the brain must maintain a chemical balance with potassium ions inside the cells and calcium ions on the outside. Neurotransmitters are released at the end of axons. **Neuron following concussion *(bottom)*:** Communication between nerve cells is impaired. The chemical balance in the brain is turned upside down. Potassium ions flood out of cells, and calcium ions rush inside. Neurotransmitters are chaotically released. Nerve cells are alive but essentially paralyzed, unable to transmit impulses.

pump the ions back to the right places, the brain needs energy. But the chemical imbalances resulting from the concussion hinder that process, slowing or preventing the metabolic processes. At a time when the brain needs energy to set itself straight, its ability to make energy is greatly impaired.

David Hovda, a well-regarded research scientist at UCLA, has studied these chemical imbalances in laboratory rats. Dr. Hovda's research points out that while cell chemistry in rats is disrupted for a short time after a concussion, it takes longer to return to normal. That reversal may occur over weeks, even months. Assuming that our brains function exactly as the brains of rats is quite a leap — and likely inaccurate. Still, it is worth thinking about these findings and what they reveal about concussed athletes.

Symptoms

All concussions are accompanied by symptoms. They fall into four major categories:

> **Somatic:** Headaches, nausea, vomiting, balance and/or visual problems, dizzy spells, and issues such as sensitivity to light and noise.
> **Emotional:** Sadness to the point of depression (even suicide), nervousness, and irritability.
> **Sleep disturbance:** Sleeping more or less than usual and trouble falling asleep.
> **Cognitive:** Difficulty concentrating, troubles with memory, feeling mentally slow or as if in a fog that will not lift.

The first time I see patients, I ask them to complete a symptom checklist, a three-page form on which twenty-six symptoms associated with concussions are listed (see Appendix A, page 163). The symptoms are listed in alphabetical order starting with "balance issues" all the way to "trouble falling asleep" and "visual problems." In between are a range of symptoms, some commonly associated with concussions — fatigue, feeling in a fog, headache, problems with memory and concentration, sensitivity to light and noise — and others less common, such as ringing in the ears and vomiting. We ask our patients to tell us which of the symptoms they have experienced and to rank them by severity. In addition, patients complete a similar form that records symptoms they suffered with any past concussions (see Appendix B, page 165) and, thirdly, a medical history form (see Appendix C, page 167). This is how it might work on the form noting past concussions. If a young person had previous head trauma, the instruction would be, for concussion number one, put a "1" here noting that the symptoms affected balance issues only and "2" beside it to show that the symptoms were moderate. For the second concussion, the only symptom was confusion and it was relatively mild. The patient puts a "2-1" in the appropriate box for the second concussion. For each of the previous concussions, I'm able to calculate what is called a symptom load — the total number of concussion symptoms he's had for each concussion, and a symptom score based on the severity of the symptoms. Most important, when they come in, patients go through a similar process letting me know about their symptoms that day. I have a symptom load and scale for that visit and every future visit. In addition, I ask the patient to tell me how many times he's had the symptoms without a concussion being diagnosed. For many, the number may exceed recognized concussions by more than fivefold.

Under past medical history, I also record conditions that can negatively affect concussion recovery and prevent one from being asymptomatic after full recovery from the concussion. Such conditions include attention deficit disorder (ADD), attention deficit hyperactivity disorder (ADHD), other learning disorders, depression, anxiety disorders or panic attacks, and migraine headaches.

Symptoms are clues. They reveal many things — the severity of the injury and the pace of recovery, for example. The number and combination also can pinpoint areas of the brain affected by a concussion. Those that are focal — the insult is to one area — tend to result in fewer symptoms of shorter duration. When trauma is diffuse — spread across several regions — the patient has more symptoms that persist longer. Take the case of a hockey player who falls on the ice and cracks his head. If the blow affected the medial temporal lobe (controlling thought, attention, memory, and so on) and the calcarine cortex (affecting vision) located in the medial back of the brain, there would be multiple symptoms.

When will my child be *over* her concussion? When will I be *better*? These are questions that every patient and every parent of every patient wants answered. There is no "normal" recovery for a child with a concussion — no timeline or timetable to predict when symptoms will lift. In approximately 80 percent of concussion patients, symptoms clear within seven to ten days. In 20 percent of cases, the patient feels the effects for a longer period, sometimes much longer. Symptoms can last for weeks or months or, in a few cases, years. In a chapter on post-concussion syndrome we will learn about these cases in detail. We'll review the reasons that mild concussions become more serious ones and the consequences when they do. Some kids have to leave school for a year. Others have to give up one collision sport that they really enjoy or, even worse, all competitive sports.

Rest

Rest is the hallmark of concussion therapy. The best we can do for patients is to shut things down physically and cognitively. That doesn't mean going into a dark room and staying in bed. That would ruin the rest of your body. Generally speaking, it means reducing the thinking and reasoning in a patient's life as much as needed so that symptoms are not provoked. We start with restrictions at school. If paying attention in class makes symptoms worse, the student shouldn't be in class or should be on a modified schedule of classes. If taking a one-hour exam exacerbates symptoms, the child needs to refrain from such tests. Outside school, patients should virtually eliminate anything that's intellectually stimulating. This includes any activity that involves staring at a screen or a page: text messaging, Facebook-ing, TV, movies, and outside recreational reading.

When a patient isn't doing well, we continue to reduce cognitive load. We turn the dial a half crank until the patient has reached a point at which she is functioning without symptoms being provoked. It can take several attempts to find this level. In some patients, it can mean recommending that the young person withdraw from virtually all that had defined her life before the injury.

School attendance can be a highly emotional issue because of all it encompasses in a child's life.

Taking away the young person's sport is bad enough. Coping with the common twenty-six post-concussion symptoms making him feel absolutely miserable is bad enough. Taking him out of school for an extended period, perhaps an entire school year, is another blow. For many, it is sober confirmation that their lives are on indefinite hold. Their classmates are graduating at a certain time and they're not. It adds a hurdle to their recovery at a time when they do not need one.

These situations are complicated for the patients and the doctors. We are asking these young athletes to walk the thinnest of tightropes. On one hand, we do not want them to lose a school year. On the other, the cognitive activity inherent in attending school is hurting their recovery. There is a balance, and we try to find it.

Why Children Are Vulnerable

There's considerable research to support the proposition that a child's brain takes longer to recover from concussion than an adult's brain. Most of these studies deal with high school athletes; that limits the conclusions we can draw about younger kids. Yet what is known points to children being at risk.

Not surprisingly, the comparison centers on key developmental differences between adults and children. There are several worth emphasizing, all bearing directly on the brain's response to trauma. Myelin is the fat that covers the fiber tracts in the brain. Think of a copper wire inside the wall of your house and of the plastic or rubber coating around the wire. The coating insulates, protects, and strengthens that wire. The fiber tracks of adults have a coating of myelin that acts in the same way, protecting the fibers from injury or insult. Brain trauma still can occur, of course. But myelination is an excellent defense. Children's brains have less myelin, so structures in their brains are more easily damaged.

A child's brain and head are disproportionately large for the rest of the body, especially through the first five to eight years of life. It's true up through about the age of fourteen, by which time a child's skull has grown to be about 90 percent as large as an adult-size one. That may sound like trivia, but it's important to a discussion of concussions and concussion risk. The extra size and weight, coupled with a child's weaker neck, mean that the child can't brace for a hit the way an adult does. Rotational forces will be greater for a child, proportional to the severity of the hit. The hit itself may not generate the same force because of the speed of the collision and the weights of the (junior) players involved, but what is transferred to the head may be as great or greater. It's all about neck strength.

Total brain trauma is the worry regarding child athletes. If you start accumulating injuries early in life, chances are that you will have a greater number of them during your life. It's unclear what the effects of that long-term repetitive trauma might be. The philosophy I preach to my patients is as follows: No head trauma is good head trauma. If knocking around the brain can be avoided, then avoid it. This is my mantra even though there are many blanks to fill in regarding our knowledge of head trauma and its true effects. One concern is that kids who are playing in a tackle football league at age five (yes, such leagues exist) or engaged in another rough-and-tumble sport are at risk of a degenerative brain disease, chronic traumatic encephalopathy. CTE has been detected in the brains of many adult football and hockey players and in the brains of several teenagers. We know that total brain trauma (concussions and subconcussive blows) is a risk factor for CTE. Beyond brain trauma, what allows one person to have CTE and another person not to is for now unknown.

Recognizing Concussions

If you played competitive sports as a child, you know that concussions were thought to be not that serious. Few leagues educated coaches. There literally were no rules regarding concussions. It basically was up to the youth player to decide whether he was injured and should come out of the game. In many cases, a coach would ask a player, "Are you all right?" If the answer was yes, the player went back in.

Thirty years ago, even medical personnel received little guidance. Basic protocols were left up to individual schools, teams, athletic trainers, and physicians. If a player had a concussion, what were the restrictions? Was it safe for that player to play in the next game? To return to *that* game? There were lots of opinions and methods of treatment.

In 1986, I published the first "Return to Play" guidelines in a peer-reviewed journal, *Physician and Sports Medicine,* with the intention of moving toward a universal standard (see Appendix D, page 169). Over the years, these guidelines became an integral part of the care received by athletes. They classified concussions by grades one, two, and three, three being the most severe. At each grade, there were recommendations as to how the player should be handled. A player with a grade two concussion, for instance, was held out a minimum of two weeks if he was symptom-free for seven days. A player with a grade three concussion whose trauma caused him to lose consciousness for minutes was out for at least a month. The "Return to Play" protocol was intended to augment, not replace, clinical judgments. Decisions about how to care for an injured player remain with medical personnel on the scene, and always should. In the decades since the first guidelines, more than thirty alternatives have been published. In 2001, the "Return to Play" protocol was updated and sharpened. Now a player who reports a single concussion symptom is not permitted to return to that game.

More than thirty states now have laws that incorporate a similar principle, known as "When in Doubt, Sit Them Out." Under "When in Doubt," if a player shows signs of being drowsy or confused, or has another concussion symptom, that player is out for the rest of that game, end of discussion. In addition, the player cannot be left alone (out of concern that her condition could deteriorate). Before being allowed to return to the game, the athlete must be cleared by a doctor or other medical personnel trained in concussion recognition and management.

Some of the most ardent supporters of "When in Doubt, Sit Them Out" are athletes — often young athletes. When the Minnesota state legislature was debating a bill that embraced this standard, Kayla Meyer was one of the first to testify. Kayla had been playing ice hockey since she was three years old. At age fifteen, she'd suffered two concussions that had kept her out of school for more than two months. She also suffered from persistent headaches.

"Players today have their mind-set that 'I'm tough and strong' whether they're a girl or a guy . . . Coaches, teammates, players, parents, team trainers, and doctors need more information about concussions and brain injuries, to help people not go through what I'm going through," Kayla told the legislators. It's hard to imagine a better endorsement of "When in Doubt, Sit Them Out."

Underreporting of Concussions

Despite our progress, challenges remain. Underreporting of concussions exists in all sports and is a special challenge in a few sports such as football and ice hockey. Football's rules and rhythms camouflage the problem. In a football game, there is more "stop time" than "go time" — thirty seconds between plays, four or five seconds for the average play. A player who gets knocked silly has a few seconds to recover, remember where he is, and get back to the huddle. Unless he's the quarterback, he isn't speaking in the huddle. He's wearing a huge helmet. No one can look into his eyes if they're trying, which they probably aren't. Line up these factors and a running back might be able to play a series or even a half before it is discovered he was playing impaired.

Underreporting of concussions in youth ice hockey has been documented in several studies; a recently published one suggests the problem is significant. The study's primary author is Dr. Paul Echlin, a physician from London, Ontario, who worked with researchers from an organization called the Hockey Concussion Education Program. Dr. Echlin and his colleagues followed two junior hockey teams in Ontario throughout the 2009–10 season. These were highly competitive teams — a number of players hoped to graduate to college hockey programs. The players' ages ranged from sixteen to twenty-one.

The purpose of the study was simple enough: to track the number of concussions reported among the players on the two teams. Just as important, Dr. Echlin was looking for evidence of possible concussions that were missed by either coaches, medical personnel, or the players themselves. Or simply ignored.

When it was released in 2010, the study garnered a great deal of attention; the findings were that alarming. Foremost was that ice hockey is a much more dangerous game than was previously thought, at least more dangerous the way it was being played by the two teams in Dr. Echlin's study.

An earlier study looking at NCAA Division I programs had reported a rate of 3.1 concussions per 1,000 man-games. The Echlin study, observing athletes of roughly the same age playing exactly the same sport, found a rate nearly seven times greater than that — 21.5 concussions per 1,000 man-games.

It was more troubling than just the greater number. The Echlin study described a culture in which concussions were not treated as a serious health issue or, it seemed, an issue at all. Players described being under pressure from their coaches to continue playing even when they'd been told by medical professionals that they'd suffered concussions and should take time off. The attitudes of some parents were even more puzzling. One told the research team that it should leave the team and let his child go back to thinking about hockey instead of the potential for injury: "He needs to play on instincts and can't be worried about getting a concussion every time he goes into a corner." The researchers might have heard more comments like that had they been allowed to complete the season with both teams — they weren't. The general manager of one pulled his team out of the study midway through the season, telling the researchers that he didn't want his players submitting to in-game examinations anymore.

An interesting angle of the study is the way in which the researchers collected information. At the hockey games, physician observers were placed in the stands. When one saw somebody get up slowly or noticed that a player seemed stunned from a blow, the observer would note it and between periods go to the locker room to examine the player involved. The examinations often turned up concussions that coaches, players, and on-the-bench medical personnel themselves had overlooked. For every concussion picked up by coaches and players, the physician observers picked up seven. *Seven.*

On the Sidelines

On the sidelines, the job of the physician or athletic trainer is to decide whether there is any doubt. The coach shares responsibility. If he or she has any concerns about a particular player, the kid should be pulled. For the doctor, the evaluation is a matter of looking into the eyes of the player and asking a series of questions. In this situation, I'm looking for clues that the individual knows what's going on around her. If she's not responding appropriately to simple questions, there are issues.

Questions I would use are these: *What was the play you were injured on? What was the color of the jerseys of the opposing team?* (I don't let them turn around to look.) *What quarter is it? What's the score?* These things reveal whether the athlete is alert to what was going on at the time of the injury. Of course, there's always the simplest question of all: *Do you remember what happened?*, followed by *Tell me what you recall.*

If they're getting through the simple stuff, I'll move on to other cognitive tests. I give them six digits and ask them to repeat them, then to repeat them backwards. Then a simple balance test: Can the player stand firm with their feet together, in heel-to-toe tandem position, and on one foot, eyes open and then closed; with hands on hips, eyes open and then closed?

The age of the athlete is important to take into account. There's not a huge difference between evaluating an adult and evaluating a young athlete, say nine or ten years old. Yet there is a difference with very young kids. It's necessary to explain more, and perhaps use more care about the language used. You have to be clear — and they have to be clear — about the meaning of words. For example, a young child probably won't know about being "dinged" and would be confused by a term such as "feeling in a fog" — both are slang for being conked on the head. Some will know "dazed" and some won't. The key is to communicate on a level that is understood by the athlete, whatever the age.

Sideline evaluations aren't foolproof. Occasionally, a player who has a concussion is tested and cleared to return to the game. It quickly becomes clear that there's a problem. A colleague at the University of Florida shared one of the more dramatic examples I've heard.

The story concerned a player on the University of Florida football team and a game in Gainesville, where conditions can be rough, especially the heat and humidity. As a result, dehydration, heat illness, and heat stroke are always issues of concern. This is important to note because early symptoms of dehydration and heat illness, before they progress to heat stroke, can be quite similar to symptoms of a concussion — headache, confusion, and feeling lightheaded.

During the game, my colleague was asked to assess an athlete who'd just come off the field. He sat down with the player and gave him a thorough evaluation. The athlete appeared fine. After ten minutes, he was cleared to go back in.

The player got in the game as a punt returner. He fielded the ball and returned it a few yards. As he came off the field again, the team doctor asked him about the punt he'd just caught. The player replied, "What punt?" He had no recall whatsoever.

These situations are rare, fortunately. Our ability to recognize concussions and protect players who've had them has improved markedly. There's lots of room for improvement, though, as we will see over the following pages.

2

Collision Sports

Any parent who has let their child play football in the past fifty years
and claimed never to have understood the risks involved was either
kidding himself or an idiot.

— BUZZ BISSINGER (*Huffington Post*)

A NUMBER OF YEARS AGO, I was invited to speak to a high
school football program in the Boston area. The invitation
came from the coach, whom I also knew from his visits to my office.
He'd been a surgical patient of mine. I'd also operated on his wife. We
knew each other well and had mutual respect.

This man was an outstanding coach and a hard-working guy. He
also took youth football very seriously. Though he was a teacher and
coached at the local high school, he kept a very close eye on the crop
of talent coming up through the Pop Warner and middle school programs. Any kid who was really good and enthusiastic about football
was urged to keep playing and discouraged from going off to soccer
or another sport.

The Pop Warner team, I learned, operated as something of a
feeder system for the high school. At the Pop Warner level, players were already learning the lingo that would be used on the high
school team. They were even running many of the same plays. It
was all unofficial, of course. But this quasi farm system seemed to
be quite effective. The high school program was a powerhouse and
had won a number of conference and state super bowl titles for this
coach.

This background helps to explain the startling situation I walked into on the afternoon that I gave my presentation to his team, which included a brief speech and an informational video about football and head trauma prepared by the National Athletic Trainers' Association. Afterward I responded to questions — nothing out of the blue or surprising. But as I was leaving, the coach who'd extended the invitation approached and thanked me for coming, then added, "But I don't think we'll need you to come back again." His tone was very courteous, but also firm.

I was taken totally off-guard. For the previous hour, I'd spoken about keeping kids safe. Wasn't that a message he wanted his players to hear every season?

The coach explained that though what I'd said was important, he didn't want to frighten his players. Apparently I'd made a few squeamish, thinking about the possibility of a head injury, and he didn't want squeamish players.

That experience underscores the contradictions in our approach to football and ice hockey for kids. These are the sports in which smashing into your opponent isn't just a possibility — it's the object of the game. In both sports, I see the seeds of change for the better. Adults truly are getting the message that (I'm repeating myself) no head trauma is good head trauma. In both, more voices every day are calling for meaningful change.

But for every yin, there is a yang. There are still people and organizations in the youth sports community who do not — or are unwilling to — see the dangers. But it's my job, and my passion, to open an honest dialogue about the sports that we love and how we can make them safer if we commit ourselves to putting the interests of our children first.

Ice Hockey

Ice hockey is a great sport for kids. At any age, a child on a hockey team is getting plenty of aerobic exercise. As a bonus, they're acquiring a skill that they will value all their lives. Go to a skating rink and be on the lookout for the strongest skaters. Chances are good that at some point they were hockey players.

Hockey also is a collision sport that exposes players to an unusually high risk of head trauma. Playing conditions inherently present all sorts of hazards. The ice is hard. The boards circling the ice are hard. Until recently, rules of youth hockey have allowed for considerable contact. In our office, we see dozens of patients each winter for concussions caused by aggressive play with shoulders and sticks and from players sliding across the ice and banging their head. The hard contact also can cause injury to the cervical spine, causing paralysis.

More research is needed on head trauma in youth hockey, but the data that is available supports the idea that kids playing the sport are vulnerable. Several colleagues from Canada have done important work supporting these ideas. In 2009, the researchers Ian Williamson of the University of British Columbia and David Goodman of Simon Fraser University published a paper in the *Journal of ASTM International*, finding that among players suffering concussions, 34 percent were returning to play in the same game — an alarming rate.

Charles Tator has been a concussions oracle for a decade. Tator is a triple threat — a neurosurgeon, researcher, and tireless advocate for safety in sports. In 1992, he established ThinkFirst Canada, now ThinkFirst.ca, as an education soapbox. Its work is varied and has been making an impact in many ways. Once a year, ThinkFirst stages Brain Day, when scientists, university students, parents, and kids join in teaching and learning.

The leadership of youth hockey is progressive and unafraid to confront the crisis of head trauma. Recently, USA Hockey and Hockey Canada, the two most powerful governing bodies in the sport, demonstrated their leadership. Hockey Canada outlawed checking to the head at any level of amateur hockey. That reversed a decades-old tradition of kids teeing off on each other and doing so within the rules. The board of USA Hockey also turned the page and approved a ban on body checking before the age of thirteen, thereby raising the ban on body checking by two years. (The previous rule permitted body checking in the Pee Wee Division, comprising ages eleven and twelve.)

Announcing the change in January 2011, USA Hockey stated that the ban would eliminate "intimidation-type blowup hits resulting in head trauma among younger players." In addition, the new rules would grow better players. Hitting in youth hockey had become a distraction. Instead of learning to handle a stick and to be a competent skater, kids studied how to knock other kids down (or avoid being knocked over first). One USA Hockey official went so far as to describe the checking ban as "a skill development initiative first."

Youth hockey is a safer sport for the checking restrictions — that's beyond dispute. Fewer kids will fall on the ice and knock their heads, lowering the rate of concussions. It follows logically that the measures also will lift participation in hockey. Parents' ambivalence about a sport known (and feared) for the risk of brain injury will be overcome, and more will happily sign up their kids at the local rink.

Despite those benefits, the announcement hasn't pleased everyone. Before the rule took effect, parents and coaches objected for competitive reasons. Kids playing in USA Hockey programs would be at a disadvantage against leagues in which kids have been taught since their earliest days on skates to play rough, according to some who were displeased. As a consequence, their children would be falling behind other kids learning the finer points of checking before they turned twelve. I've even heard detractors object to the no-checking rule on grounds that it would have the unintended effect of encouraging girls to remain in boys' hockey programs longer than in the past. Body checking isn't permitted in all-girls hockey leagues. The thinking goes that the new rule will delay for a few years the switch of some girls from mostly boys leagues to all-girls programs. In turn, that will siphon players from these excellent girls' teams.

Change is hard, and especially change to a sport such as hockey, which parents want their children to experience as they did when they were young and taking body checks on the neighborhood fish pond. I have no intent to trivialize these concerns. Rather, the point

I am making is that preserving the past is not acceptable when the price is so high.

In a better world, the National Hockey League would be an example to all in hockey for its progressive stance in dealing with head trauma. Yet the NHL's current policy regarding hits to the head is complicated and disappointing. Under the rules, blind-side hits are banned. When a player doesn't see a hit coming, he cannot legally be hit in the head. That's clearly beneficial. The league has adopted a rule to discourage hits that the player *sees* coming. (A hit that targets the head is illegal.) But come on. That's marginally better than no rule at all. The penalty for such behavior is barely a slap — two minutes of short-handed skating for the offending team. And how in the world do officials determine which hits to the head are "targeted"? The answer is, they don't. This rule is rarely enforced, contributing to the perception on the ice that almost anything goes.

To its credit, the league sometimes rights a wrong. During the NHL Playoffs in April 2012, the Phoenix Coyotes player Raffi Torres wiped out Marian Hossa of the Chicago Blackhawks with a blow to the head so violent that Hossa had to be taken from the ice on a stretcher. (He had sustained a concussion.) Incredibly, the game officials made no call. Brendan Shanahan, the NHL's vice president of player safety, reviewed videotape of the collision and acted decisively, perhaps because Torres is a habitual offender with five previous infractions. The player received a twenty-five-game suspension.

I acknowledge that there is a difference between the hit you see coming and the one you don't. The blind-side hit is more dangerous because the player's neck is lax, not tensed, and that impairs a player's ability to steady the head and reduce the effect of the collision. Therefore, the player hit from the blind side is more vulnerable.

For evidence of the inadequacy of the NHL's policy, look no further than the 2010–11 season and the shortened year of Sidney Crosby, the Pittsburgh Penguins' superstar. Crosby sat out the final four months after a concussion in January. This wasn't the only or even the most serious injury to a player that season. Max Pacioretty of the Montreal Canadiens suffered a broken neck after plowing into a support stanchion in a collision with a Boston Bruins player.

Hockey players, coaches, and executives are known as a tough bunch. After what happened to Crosby and other players in a brutal season of injuries, the stoicism faded. A few questioned whether the rules were adequate to protect the players from themselves.

"This thing is running us over and we're not stopping it," said Pat LaFontaine, an NHL great who was forced to retire with head injuries, to the *Sporting News*. "Players are continually having to retire because of head injuries. You have to put a stop to it. God forbid if it's Sidney Crosby next."

The Penguins general manager Ray Shero also called for the league to take action, particularly regarding hits to the head. "My position is there should be no head hits," he told the *New York Times*. Shero dismissed objections that eliminating hits to the head would detract from the fabric of the game.

"There's over 50,000 hits in a year. If there's 10 or 20 questionable ones, is that going to take the fabric of our game away? If you have 49,892 hits in our game, it's not going to change it that much."

Even to a nonexpert, the issues and consequences of inaction are evident. The NHL must do more to protect the players, the players who put the fans in the arenas. It also must send a message that will filter down to every youth hockey league in the United States, Canada, and wherever kids play the sport. That message is this: The big guys in Boston, Montreal, and Winnipeg take head trauma very seriously. How about you?

The commissioner Gary Bettman shoulders much of the responsibility for the league's inadequate response. I've been critical of Bettman for not doing enough to protect NHL players. Those comments have been based largely on statements of his I've read in the *New York Times* and other press accounts. Recently, I had a chance to meet privately with Commissioner Bettman. I haven't changed my mind. But I was encouraged by what I heard. He grasped the issue far better than I'd thought.

Football

Five years ago the National Football League was in a state of denial about head trauma in its game. Today, it's a force for change. The difference between then and now is the current commissioner, Roger Goodell.

I have professional connections to the NFL and they should be disclosed here. I serve as a senior advisor to the NFL's Head, Neck, and Spine Committee. During collective bargaining negotiations in 2012, I was consulted on a league proposal to reduce contact drills during training camp and the regular season. In addition, I had a hand in the NFL's decision to allow officials to request that a player showing signs of a head injury go to the sidelines and be checked out, and also to have an NFL official high in the stadium making similar determinations.

The NFL has generously supported Boston University's Center for the Study of Traumatic Encephalopathy, of which I am a co-director. In 2010, the league donated $1 million to the center to support our work exploring links between repeated head trauma over many years and CTE. The money is given without strings.

Goodell exemplifies how one person can have a huge impact on player safety if that person has the power and the will. The converse is also true. A foot-dragger in the same position can be an obstacle that can't be overcome. Paul Tagliabue, Goodell's predecessor, retired in 2006 after seventeen years in the top spot. Tagliabue, a Washington lawyer, oversaw exponential growth in the game in TV revenues, stadium development, and above all fan interest. Awareness of the head trauma crisis rose during Tagliabue's last years in the job. But the NFL's response was to have little response. Relying on a small group of advisors, the organization rejected the idea that football had any connection to degenerative brain injury. Tagliabue never struck me as engaged by the issue. In our few meetings, he was pleasant, businesslike, and incurious.

Goodell set a different tone. That was evident to me the first time we met. The occasion was a medical meeting convened by the NFL. I had been asked to speak about the league's (to that point) unwillingness to acknowledge a link between head trauma and later-life cognitive problems of former players. For months, I had publicly questioned the NFL's handling of the situation. Under the circumstances, the introduction could have been awkward and strained. Instead, Goodell immediately thanked me for caring for Ted Johnson, a former NFL player who was suffering from post-concussion syndrome, and made no mention that I had been knocking the league. I've since learned through experience that he keeps an open mind.

Goodell is a doer, and at his direction the NFL has done a lot. Players with symptoms of concussion are barred from returning to practice or games. Those diagnosed with a concussion must be cleared by an outside independent neurological consultant in addition to the team physician before returning to practice. Players absorb fewer blows to the head since the league and players agreed on a reduced schedule of full-contact drills.

On Goodell's watch, tackling rules also have been amended, tipping decisively to protect "defenseless" players. When a pass receiver hauls in a throw and is still in a vulnerable position in midair, a defender isn't allowed to smash his head or neck. It's an impressive start. Now the NFL needs to take all intentional hitting to the head out of the sport.

Goodell has a conscience, and that partly explains the pace of change. He also is looking out for the NFL. He understands that the league prospers by putting the best product on the field for every game. In other words, the best players. No one wants to see the game stopped for ten minutes while their favorite player is taken off the field on a stretcher and all the players kneel in prayer on the sidelines. Okay, maybe a few nutcases enjoy that scene. The vast majority of fans want the players healthy and on the field, where they can do thrilling things.

The NFL is on the leading edge of change occurring throughout football. An encouraging shift also is taking place in the college game. In 2011, the Ivy League became the first conference to reduce full-contact practices and workouts. The Ivy's eight schools agreed to two full-contact workouts per week during the season and restrictions during preseason.

The league wants to go further, and formed a committee to reduce head trauma in other contact sports, including ice hockey and lacrosse — a committee I serve on.

That seems progressive until you look at St. John's University in the tiny town of Collegeville, Minnesota. The Johnnies' football coach is John Gagliardi, who sets records for wins and longevity every time he steps on the field. That happens when you're well into your seventh decade of coaching college football. Coach Gagliardi has notched more victories than any college football coach in history, approaching five hundred. His teams have won national championships four times. He is one of two active coaches in the College Football Hall of Fame. (The other is Chris Ault of the University of Nevada.)

An equally important part of this coach's legacy is his no-tackling policy — tackling and hard contact aren't permitted during the Johnnies' workouts. Potentially brain-rattling hits are reserved for games. It has been that way for a long time on Coach Gagliardi's team.

"We haven't had a tackle on our field since 19 . . . I'd say 56," he explained. "We do everything you do in a game except tackling, except bringing a guy down," Coach Gagliardi doesn't consider himself to be a pioneer. He doesn't even see his unorthodox methods as having a lot to do with lowering the risk of CTE. He's just using common sense and trying to protect his players.

The coach adds, "We're always in shoulder pads and helmets in our practices. We line up as if it's a game situation most of the time, with eleven players on each side of the ball. When the whistle blows, it's a full go except" — here's where Coach Gagliardi has been ahead of the curve for many years — "when we get to the ball carrier we don't bring him down like we're tackling. We'll just go into him a bit. Then we stop."

When Coach Gagliardi put this system into place, President

Eisenhower was in office. The Dodgers were still in Brooklyn. Most of today's head coaches in the NFL had yet to be born. Few physicians were talking about the dangers of head trauma in football. I asked him how the idea to remove tackling from practices had come to him. He explained that the idea began when he was a high school football player in the 1940s.

"We had a traditional coach who did things the way everyone did at the time. Practices were very demanding, very physical. As a player you learned to take the punishment, but it never made sense to me. Injuries were common. It seemed senseless. I began thinking that if I ever had an opportunity to coach, I would do things my way."

When he took over a high school team in 1943, one of the first things he did was to eliminate tackling in practice. The players worked on the skills involved in tackling as they had before. But they stopped short of clobbering their teammates. They saved that for the game.

Coach Gagliardi did not stop there. "Coaches at the time thought that it was a terrible idea during a strenuous workout to drink water. I figured that was impossible. Why wouldn't you allow a thirsty person to drink? At first, the players literally were afraid to drink. We'd take a break and I would be the only one drinking. The players could not be convinced that it was safe. Eventually, we won them over. In light of everything we know now about hydration, it's hard to believe, isn't it?"

St. John's and its trailblazing coach cannot prove that their football players have fewer injuries in practices than players at other schools. They're not seeking publicity or measuring themselves against other college teams. "We're not trying to convert anybody," Coach Gagliardi says. "We're just trying to survive."

Yet it's evident that players on his team spend less time in the trainer's room than do their counterparts on other college football teams. I asked about Johnnies players injured during the previous season. He hesitated a moment before replying, "One of our stars got hurt because he jumped out of a bunk bed. We had another guy who injured himself changing a tire." If a player had been hurt in practice, he forgot to mention it.

St. John's and the Ivy League schools are outliers for now. Will they be outliers in five years from now, or two — even next season? For all their wisdom, neither St. John's (a Division III program) nor Ivy League football (offering no athletic scholarships) is a collegiate power. Whether Auburn, Alabama, Oklahoma, and other national championship contenders embrace non- and reduced-contact practices is for now an open question. My hunch — and hope — is that such an era in college football is about to begin. Within a year of this book's publication, at least one major conference will adopt a reduced-contact practice policy.

Football at the youth level is the greatest challenge by far. Children are among the most vulnerable to injury because they have weak necks and immature musculature, and their brains are still developing. And youth football by far accounts for the largest number of players — almost three million from ages six to fourteen, according to USA Football. Pop Warner Scholars is one of the largest and most widely known organizations in not just youth football but all youth sports. Millions of kids have played on a Pop Warner football team since the program's founding in Philadelphia in the 1920s as a plan to rehabilitate mischievous boys. (Pop Warner also runs cheerleading squads.)

Playing team sports is worthwhile for kids, regardless of age. Team sports teach lessons that can't be learned in an individual game such as tennis or golf. In football, a lineman can execute a crackerjack block that clears the way for the runner to burst through the hole. The runner trips on his feet and the play ends with no gain. Or the opposite occurs and we mess up at the expense of teammates. That's analogous to real life, isn't it? We do the best we can, expect colleagues to give their best effort, and live with the outcome no matter what.

Pop Warner has approximately 285,000 players on football teams and launches the careers of many who go on to play with their high school teams on Friday nights, not to mention the select few whose talent and hard work carry them to the college and pro ranks. The organization isn't above questioning and criticism, though. Pop Warner football can be highly competitive and narrowly focused on winning — too focused, given that some of the players are four feet tall. Each season ends with a Pop Warner Super Bowl played at ESPN Walt Disney Wide World of Sports Complex in Lake Buena Vista, Florida. In 2010, the title game between the Overton Rattlers (Florida) and the Detroit Dolphins (Michigan) was televised on ESPN2. This followed the national championship game of the Junior PeeWee League for players eight, nine, and ten years old. Should third-graders compete in a national championship of anything?

Even younger players suit up for Pop Warner football. For years, the organization had teams for children starting at age five. These teams competed in flag football, a safer alternative to rougher tackle rules in which kids grab flags — rather than each other — to stop a ball carrier. Since 2005, Pop Warner added a new option for five-year-old football prospects — the Little Mite division, a full-contact tackle league. Approximately 16,000 players nationally are playing Little Mite today, and the numbers rise each year. Meanwhile, Pop Warner's flag football program for young children is stagnant.

Tackle football for five-year-olds is an idea I disapprove of in the strongest terms. This would be the place in the book to cite an article in a medical journal explaining the precise dangers of organized tackle football to the brains of young children, but this cultural phenomenon is so new that it has yet to be studied. We simply cannot gauge the long-term effects for these little ones. That alone is reason to keep children so young off the gridiron.

Pop Warner deserves mixed reviews for its response to the head trauma crisis. In 2012, the program announced reforms: Contact drills are now limited to one-third of practice time and some especially violent head-on blocking and tackling drills are banned. These are positive signs. Less impressive are the unsubstantiated statements that the program has made about the safety record of its program. Specifically, I refer to injury data posted on the organization website that likely is viewed by millions of parents and other interested adults every year.

> The injury rate in Pop Warner Football is less than one-third the injury rate in high school football [and] less than one-fifth the injury rate in college football [and] less than one-ninth the injury rate in professional football.
>
> Furthermore, Pop Warner's age-weight schematic protects younger, lighter players, who do not have higher injury rates.
>
> The Institute of Sports Medicine and Athletic Trauma in New York completed a Pop Warner injury survey in 71 towns covering over 5,000 players in 1998. The injury experience of 5,128 boys (8 to 15 years of age, weight 22.5 to 67.5 kg [50 to 150 lb]) participating in youth football revealed an overall rate of significant injury of 5%, with 61% classified as moderate and 38.9% as major injuries. That's about 1.33 per team per year. No catastrophic injuries occurred, and it was rare for a permanent disability to result from any injury.

Statements like these obscure a key fact: Pop Warner officials have no way to count the concussions occurring in their leagues. No one possibly could until trained medical personnel are present at youth football games.

A few years ago, my colleague at the Sports Legacy Institute, Chris Nowinski, and I came up with a proposal. We wanted to work with a Pop Warner league to do a concussion research study. Our plan was to monitor every game during a Pop Warner season. A certified athletic trainer would be stationed on the sidelines to evaluate kids who the coaches and parents suspected might have had a concussion. In addition, we also launched a concussion education program for the kids, parents, and coaches. We were interested in gauging the effect of education on the number of reported concussions. Were more reported when people knew what to look for and were familiar with concussion symptoms?

For the study's home base we picked a town near Boston that was a good fit in all respects. Then we approached Pop Warner officials there, presenting our proposal and making clear that this would be done at no cost to them. Everything — time, medical equipment, and so on — would be donated.

The study never happened. League officials hemmed and hawed. Finally, they told us they wanted to think it over for a year. That was a few years ago. Still no study. The fact of the matter is, Pop Warner's data about its safety record is incomplete, and until the organization opens the door to scientific study, there is still no truth.

Boxing

Recently, the American Academy of Pediatrics, the respected organization of children's doctors, published a policy statement recommending that pediatricians "vigorously oppose" boxing for any child or adolescent. The statement notes that boxing has supporters who cite its benefits. Boxers learn self-defense. Boxing builds character in children. Boxers develop strength, agility, and discipline. Boxing instills confidence, even fosters courage.

All of those benefits combined do not balance the harm that youngsters are exposed to when they climb into the ring, according to the AAP. "Boxing is the only sport where direct blows to the head are rewarded and the ultimate victory may be to render the opponent senseless." The AAP urges pediatricians to demand that boxing organizations give the best medical care to kids in their programs. It closes its policy statement with a plea to children's doctors: "Encourage patients to participate in alternative sports in which intentional head blows are not central to the sport."

I am a supporter of the American Academy of Pediatrics. I'm also a boxing fan. I have been a member of USA Boxing's medical commission and for many years have been a ringside physician. Boxing clearly is a high-risk sport for the small number of kids involved. (USA Boxing claimed 18,000 youngsters as members in 2008.)

I do not agree with the AAP that the best approach is to discourage boxing for all children. The advice is well intended, but it fails to account for the complex lives of children most likely to be boxers. Many of these kids come from inner cities; they're poor, and their opportunities are quite limited. There aren't any swim teams or baseball leagues in their neighborhoods. There may not be any swimming pools or baseball diamonds.

Boxers are seriously injured in the ring and sometimes they die. That's a fact. Not long ago, I sat at my computer searching for information about boxers killed *outside* the ring. It turned out that the cause of death most common among professional boxers was not being slugged during a bout, but being shot or stabbed in a nightclub or in the 'hood between visits to the gym. I'm not an advocate of boxing for children. The next twelve times patients ask whether boxing is a safe sport for kids, I will say no. Twelve times. I simply point out that solutions to our problems are more complicated than simply saying no to boxing.

3

Non-Collision Sports

*Why, at ages 6 [through] 11 — when your brain is still
developing — why are we heading the ball?*
— TAYLOR TWELLMAN (*Los Angeles Times*)

BILL MOREAU HAS A fascinating, and somewhat daunting,
job. As medical director of sports medicine clinics for the U.S.
Olympic Committee (USOC), Dr. Moreau oversees care for the athletes on the forty-seven teams representing the United States at the
Summer and Winter Games. That includes an Olympic team with
the astoundingly high rate of concussions: synchronized swimming.

Synchronized swimming?

I wasn't aware of the risks faced by these elite swimmers. Neither
was Dr. Moreau until recently when the women's national team arrived in Colorado Springs for a two-week training session at USOC
headquarters. Dr. Moreau hadn't provided care for synchronized
swimmers before, but during this visit he decided to serve as the
team's lead medical liaison. He remembers thinking, *It's synchronized swimming. What trouble could that be?*

Dr. Moreau soon learned exactly what trouble it could be. The national team comprised about a dozen women athletes, he said. They
trained on the USOC's campus for two weeks. During that short
period of time, half the swimmers suffered concussions. *Half.*

When we spoke months later, Dr. Moreau told me, "I was shocked.
I had no understanding that a sport we view as noncontact, non-
collision, had a concussion rate of 50 percent.

"When the average person thinks about synchronized swimming, they think attractive women doing poses in the water. They usually don't think about brain trauma.

"These women are superior athletes. They're in the pool eight hours a day. Literally, they're within inches of one another, sculling and paddling. As they go through their various routines," Bill noted, "they're literally kicking each other in the head."

Having discovered that concussions are not only an issue in synchronized swimming but a major one, the USOC is reassessing concussion awareness and prevention for all sports. On the athletes' side, the focus will be on education, because, Dr. Moreau says, many athletes in non-collision sports "aren't thinking about head injury and don't know they've had concussions." Another important element is changing the attitudes of physicians, athletic trainers, and other medical staff. "We need to begin recognizing our own biases, our own preconceptions," Dr. Moreau said.

This story illustrates a critical point. Football, ice hockey, and a few other "collision" sports dominate the head trauma discussion. But concussion awareness and education shouldn't end there. Every sport poses concussion risk, some more, some less. We need to expand the conversation and begin talking about hidden risks in sports such as basketball, soccer, and volleyball (yes, volleyball).

There is considerable data available on concussions in high school sports. These studies offer a window into concussion rates, broken down by sport and gender. A recent study, conducted during the 2009–10 school year, included some surprising results. Football and boys' ice hockey ranked one and two for concussions, as expected. Not far behind were sports often overlooked. Number three, boys' lacrosse; four, girls' soccer; five, girls' lacrosse; six, wrestling; seven, boys' soccer; eight, girls' basketball; nine, boys' basketball.

Let's not put too much stock in these "rankings." For one thing, though this is as good a list as any, it's just one study and one snapshot. Generally speaking, football and hockey are at the top of such lists, as we'd expect. Yet in some research studies, girls' soccer and girls' ice hockey are right up there in terms of recognized concussions, which few of us would expect. The important point is that more concussions are missed than are picked up — by a long shot. The potential for overlooking concussions in non-collision sports is particularly significant because . . . who's going to notice? At a high school basketball game, there may not be an athletic trainer on the bench. Certainly there wouldn't be a team doctor in the gym for a typical midseason game. It's predictable that concussions more likely would go undetected when medical personnel are not on the scene.

Wrestling

Wrestling is something of an enigma. At the high school level, it is one of the sports in the high-risk group not only for concussion but for catastrophic brain and cervical spine injury. Almost all of those injuries happen in the act of being pile-driven into the mat. Wrestler A is "taken down" by Wrestler B. In the process, Wrestler B is flipped on his head like a top; his head is driven down into the mat. That maneuver obviously puts the head at risk of concussion or worse. It puts the neck at risk for cervical fracture or perhaps a neck injury of lesser severity. What needs to be better understood is why the heck that risk seems to go away at the college level. College wrestling, unlike high school wrestling, isn't at the high end of the spectrum.

At the college level, we believe concussion risks drop in part because a process of natural selection has occurred. The kids wrestling at the college level are the ones that survived the sport in high school. They had the right skills and right strengths, including neck strength. As a result, they have better technical ability. And they have the skeletal maturity that the kids who have gotten hurt in high school didn't have. At this point, it's a theory.

Although I see fewer wrestlers than football or hockey players, the ones I do see often have concussion symptoms that are quite serious. One patient stands out. When I met Joel Weiss, he was sixteen years old and a high school wrestler. The sport suited him well, he explained. It was physical, demanding, and there were no team-mates to turn to in the heat of a match. "It's a singular sport. It's all about you," he said. "Being a wrestler gives you the courage to take on the other challenges that occur in life. You're better prepared for almost anything. That, plus it helped me lose weight. During a season, I could drop twenty-five pounds."

Joel Weiss

Wrestling may have helped Joel deal with challenges. It also has presented a few. Before he graduated from high school, Joel had suf-fered five concussions. Mishaps on the wrestling mat accounted for four. When he was fifteen, Joel and another wrestler banged heads during a match. He soon experienced a variety of classic symptoms, including dizziness, drowsiness, excessive sleep, and fatigue and feeling as if he were in a fog. The symptoms persisted for nearly three months, longer than is typical and an indication that he likely suffered from post-concussion syndrome.

I met Joel after he'd suffered three more concussions. This time, the concussions had come in rapid succession. In a match, he was dropped on his head—the first of the three. While he was training with an assistant coach, his head slammed into the mat—the second. The next day at practice, a friend dropped Joel awkwardly on his head once again. At least, that's the story his friend told him later. "I have no recollection of that day," Joel tells me.

Looking back, Joel realizes that he should have stopped wrestling after the first concussion in that awful sequence. Instead, he headed to the wrestling room and exposed himself to more serious injury. He believed that showing up for practice and meets—no matter how bad he felt—was expected of him. "I was staggering around. I was walking in zigzags. But one of the coaches had the attitude, 'You have to fight through pain.' So that's what I thought I should be doing. Now there are rules that if you're suspected of having a head injury, you have to sit out a week, sometimes more, which we didn't have at the time," he says. "I didn't take time to get better."

When I saw Joel in my office about three weeks after the third concussion in a matter of days, he had many symptoms—dizziness, drowsiness, a headache, and sensitivity to noise. What I remember most, though, was his compromised sense of balance. In all my years of treating sports concussions, I've never seen a patient's balance as severely affected. He walked into the exam room under his own power, but with difficulty. His steps were halting and uncertain. He was grossly unsteady on his feet.

Joel's recovery took time. On my recommendation, he left school for two months. When he did go back it was in a wheelchair. Eventually, in his junior year, he progressed to a cane. Joel graduated from high school and in the fall of 2011 entered college, studying astrophysics. But he doesn't feel that he is back to his old self even now. "It's taking a while, but I feel like I'm getting better. Most doctors say the [healing] happens in plateaus. For a long time, you don't feel like you're getting better, then all of a sudden you can do something again. That's where I am."

Soccer

For many families, soccer is seen as a terrific alternative to football, the thinking being *Thank goodness I have my child in a really safe activity. She's playing soccer this year.* Parents who absolutely will not allow their children to participate in football are relieved when their kids choose soccer.

From a head trauma standpoint, soccer isn't the innocuous sport we believe it is. I'm not saying, "Don't play soccer." I'm not saying, "*Do* play football." I am stating that soccer ranks near the top among youth sports in number of recognized concussions.

In 2010, more high school soccer players suffered concussions than basketball, baseball, wrestling, and softball players combined, according to the Center for Injury Research and Policy in Columbus, Ohio. In that year, female soccer players suffered 25,953 concussions, and male players, 20,247 concussions. Compare that to basketball — boys' basketball players logged 11,013 concussions.

Most of that risk comes from one play: the act of heading the ball. When two kids (or sometimes more) leap to direct the ball with their head, a number of things can happen. From a neurological standpoint, nearly all are bad. Two heads collide. A shoulder and a head crash. An elbow and a head smash. In my practice, approximately 90 percent of patients with soccer head trauma and concussion are related to heading accidents. If heading were eliminated from soccer today, it would go from one of the riskiest sports for head trauma to one of the safest.

I urge a ban on heading in soccer until players reach age fourteen. If it were within my power, heading on every youth soccer field in America would vanish right now.

I know this is an unpopular idea with some parents and coaches. That's understandable. Removing heading from the sport would be a significant change for adults accustomed to watching and teaching the sport as it's played now. I've heard many of the reservations:

It's not real soccer. Without heading, kids are playing a
    watered-down game.

If kids don't learn heading early, they won't learn properly.

You're penalizing talented kids.

Heading doesn't cause concussions if it's taught correctly.

I agree with the last point. Heading is less risky when kids use
their head and neck correctly. The reality is that few do. Many lack
the physical maturity to head a soccer ball properly and safely. Their
bodies simply have not achieved the maturity and strength. Another
significant issue is how the game is taught to young people. Millions
of volunteer coaches make the games possible. Without them, there
would be fewer opportunities for kids to play soccer — and playing
is what it's all about. Yet few coaches are trained to teach heading.
The drills that parents and coaches come up with often are not helpful and sometimes increase the risk of injury.

I have spoken about this problem with Taylor Twellman, a professional soccer star with the New England Revolution, whom I
treated for multiple concussions. Several were the result of heading
collisions in which Taylor's skull was shaken by a defender's head or
elbow (and once with a goalie's fist). Taylor told me of his deep reservations about heading in youth soccer, and specifically about the
way it is taught to the youngest players.

"When I go to youth practices, I see drills that don't make a lot
of sense," Taylor said. "A parent will kick the ball in the air — a hard
kick — and the kid is supposed to head it. They'll do that twenty
times. I struggle to understand the thinking. One, the kid in the
game is heading once or twice. Two, the ball in the game isn't going
anywhere near the velocity that it is when the parent kicks it in practice. It doesn't serve any purpose."

About a decade ago the American Youth Soccer Organization,
one of the nation's largest and most important youth sports associations, considered a ban on heading for youth players. After much debate, the AYSO decided on a compromise — to discourage heading

for players under ten. That's a positive step that I'd like to see taken further. The real answer may lie with the International Federation of Association Football, the powerful organization that runs soccer around the world. If FIFA gets behind these changes, it may move a mountain or two.

Volleyball

Volleyball is played with a soft, forgiving ball. Players are spaced around a large, open court. The game stops every ten to fifteen seconds. It isn't the most dangerous sport from a head trauma standpoint. But concussions happen.

Many occur on spikes, the hard smashes over the net designed to quickly put away a point. At the elite level, spikes have been clocked at up to ninety miles per hour. If a player takes a spiked ball to the head, concussion is possible. Similarly, players leave their feet in volleyball, diving to return balls before hitting the court or floor. With each impact, the brain shakes inside the skull, and that can result in a concussion.

Volleyball also is a sport in which the incidence of subconcussive blows is high. These are less damaging to the brain than the heavier blows that result in concussion. But they do damage. Each time a player dives for a ball and lands on her fists or chest, her head sustains a small whiplash. Add up hundreds or even thousands of those small blows a year, and the brain is dealing with real trauma.

Basketball

More kids play basketball in America than play any other high school sport except football — 500,000 boys and 450,000 girls. So it's expected that many would be hurt on playgrounds and in gyms. A recent study suggests that while the number of basketball injuries is decreasing overall, traumatic brain injury in the sport is on the rise. In 2007, approximately 4 percent of youth basketball injuries were to the head. That was more than double the percentage ten years earlier, according to research published in the journal *Pediatrics*. Greater awareness of head trauma likely is a factor in the uptick, the researchers said. So is "an ever-increasing level of competitiveness and intensity of training and play, starting at younger ages."

Technically speaking, basketball is a non-collision sport. Players aren't permitted to run over other players. There's no blocking, tackling, or cross-checking permitted. It is a physical game, however, in which collisions are routine stuff. Concussions can occur from any combination of such contact: head to head, head to elbow, head with basketball, head with folding chair, and head with hardwood floor.

The critical aspect for the adults is to recognize that head trauma occurs in basketball and that it should be managed just as it is in the higher-risk sports: If you've had a concussion, if you're symptomatic, you cannot play. If you've had a concussion, you should not be working out in the weight room or jogging. Any activity that requires mental focus or prolonged concentration should be cut back or withheld. It may be necessary to take a break from school. In short, give the brain a rest.

I've treated a number of NBA players over the years. Almost all have reported symptoms — dizziness, fatigue, and headaches — that had troubled them for weeks or months. In virtually every case, they'd suffered concussions. They hadn't realized they'd been injured. So, of course, they did not link the symptoms to head trauma. I remember one patient explaining the mind-set. "You know," he told me, "we really don't expect concussions in basketball." They do happen, of course. And if the players continue to work out and take another hit to the head, they're more likely than not to have very prolonged symptoms.

Alyssa Blood is a classic example of how predictable yet random concussions can be in basketball. Alyssa is one of the more memorable patients I have treated in recent years — bright, attractive, ambitious, and a terrific athlete. She also has an extensive concussion history. She has suffered four, including two while playing for the women's basketball team at Brown University. The first of those basketball concussions, during Alyssa's freshman year, occurred when a player on an opposing team barreled into her. Alyssa stumbled and fell, hitting the back of her head on the hardwood court. She was held out of games for a month. The second time, thirteen months later, was a case of wrong place, wrong time. Alyssa describes the situation as "completely random bad luck." The Brown team was at the arena, on the floor, warming up for a game set to begin in a few minutes. Alyssa was running off the court with her teammates when an errant ball slipped out of the hands of a teammate and slammed her hard in the left temple. This time, her recovery took not weeks or months, but years.

"Basketball is a game in which a lot of people are playing in a small area — bodies naturally come in contact," Alyssa tells me. "That's going to result in a certain number of concussions each year. I don't see lots of rules changing that. I hope we don't get to a point where players are running around in helmets."

Baseball and Softball

We know how concussions occur in baseball and softball: They're caused by a thrown or batted ball. We also know how to protect players: Require helmets. The challenge is putting helmets on kids playing baseball and ensuring that they stay on. Because, son of a gun, any time a kid's batting helmet falls off, there is a kid on that baseball diamond at risk of head trauma.

Every youth player in every baseball league I know of steps into the batter's box wearing a helmet. Most have ear flaps. Some have protective cages, as with football helmets, to protect against facial injuries. All of that is marvelous.

When a batter becomes a base runner, that changes. Helmets have a tendency to fall off. And that is how the danger creeps in. We wouldn't think of allowing a kid to step into the batter's box without a helmet. Every coach on both benches and half the people on the bleachers would be yelling at the kid to go back and get one. Yet few of us get alarmed when the same kid becomes a base runner and right away loses his helmet. Now he's rounding the bases with no head protection. It sets up a dangerous situation that, unfortunately, I have seen play out many times.

A base runner runs out of his helmet. A shortstop or third baseman guns the balls to the next base.

A split second later, the ball hits the kid in the head. If the contact occurs in the temple where the skull is thin, the result can be a life-threatening epidural hematoma.

Let me share the story of a patient that we saw about twenty years ago. This young man was a baseball player at a high school not fifteen miles from my office at Emerson Hospital in Concord. On a spring afternoon, he and his teammates were playing another local school. The team was at bat, and the young man was a base runner. As he rounded third base and headed home, the young man's batting helmet fell off or he flipped it off. Either way, his head was exposed when the third baseman let loose with a throw that got away and clocked the runner in the right temple.

The young man scored — I remember that clearly. And despite the terrible blow, he seemed to be all right. He got to his feet and took a seat in the dugout. But within ten or fifteen minutes, he went from complaining of a severe headache — which you'd expect after being hit in the bare head — to becoming lethargic to entering a highly drowsy state. A decision was made to call 911, and when the EMTs arrived they made what turned out to be a life-saving decision — they immediately headed to the emergency room. From the ambulance they called the hospital, advising us of what had happened and the patient's apparent deterioration. "He's becoming less responsive," they told us.

When he arrived at the hospital, the pupil in his right eye — the side of his face that had been struck by the ball — was enlarged, which indicated a blood clot formed on that side. Normally, you'd like to do an imaging study — a head CT scan, typically — to confirm that. There was no time. His condition was worsening quickly. We felt that waiting another twenty-five to thirty minutes to get the scan might seal the deal in terms of a bad outcome.

The fortunate thing in this situation was that it happened late in the afternoon—five-thirty or six. I hadn't left the hospital yet and was there to assess the young man when he arrived by ambulance. Because we knew he was on his way, the OR crew was also held at the hospital and waiting. In the emergency room, he was lapsing into a coma. I took him directly to the operating room, where an epidural hematoma was removed. In forty-plus years, we've had a few cases for which we've thanked our lucky stars that everything lined up perfectly. This was one of those times. If another hour had passed, he would have died or had a serious, permanent injury. As it was, because of the quick action of the coach, the EMTs, and the hospital staff, the young man made a full recovery. He even went back to playing sports.

This story had a happy ending. Yet for me it's a reminder that youth baseball organizations should be doing more to protect players' heads. The next step is an obvious one—and, it seems to me, one that is simple to accomplish. All youth baseball organizations should require chin straps on helmets. Straps that snap securely and prevent kids from being rushed to Emerson Hospital by ambulance.

Many leagues around the country already require chin straps. One stellar example is the Par-Troy West Little League of Parsippany, New Jersey, a program that clearly puts safety first. Par-Troy requires chin straps for all players nine years old and younger in both baseball and softball. More youth leagues should follow this example.

It's also time for youth baseball leagues to ban what clearly is the most dangerous play in their sport: the headfirst slide. As far as plays that result in catastrophic head and neck injury, including concussion, number one is clearly the headfirst slide. It's not needed. It wouldn't be missed. And there really is no place for it at the youth level.

Like heading in soccer, sliding headfirst is less dangerous if done with perfect form. The problem is that kids rarely achieve perfect form in baseball or other things, and we shouldn't expect perfection from them. Little kids are going to continue to make little-kid mistakes on the base paths, sliding late, coming into the base with too much speed. When a child's head plows into an ankle or a shin, the leg always wins. Worse are home-plate collisions in which the head of the base runner crashes into the hard plastic and metal fasteners of the catcher's shin guards, collisions that exact an even greater toll.

As a former college baseball player myself, and something of a purist, I'm not trying to strip collegiate or pro baseball of the head-first slide. Youth baseball organizations, on the other hand, should ban it now.

The national organizations, including Dixie Baseball, Cal Ripken Baseball, and Little League Baseball, do a commendable job on most safety issues. Little League Baseball has taken some heat over pitching rules — critics say it has been slow to adopt rules that protect the throwing arms of young pitchers. Otherwise, it's quite progressive. In 1959, Little League mandated that kids wear batting helmets with ear flaps. A few years ago, Little League eliminated on-deck circles so that kids waiting their turn at bat wouldn't be hit by flying bats or balls, and replaced traditional bases with a breakaway model to protect players from wrapping their ankles around immovable objects.

Little League's position on headfirst slides is to ban them when runners are advancing to the next base and permit them when returning to a base. That's a good rule that could be better. So I'll say it again. No headfirst slides.

Recently, I turned on the TV and happened to catch a few innings of the Little League World Series from Williamsport, Pennsylvania. I was thrilled by what I saw — as only someone in my profession would be. Every batter in the game wore a bulky, somewhat unfashionable batting helmet. What the helmet lacks in style points, it more than makes up for in protection from head trauma. I recognized the model as a cutting-edge design that incorporates a thin outer layer of polycarbonate.

Baseball players of all levels should be wearing helmets with these upgrades. In the professional ranks, they've been shunned. Citing their uncoolness, when they cite anything at all, big-leaguers have refused to wear them.

Cheerleading

By far, the riskiest position on any cheer team is the flyer. For those unfamiliar with the term, this is the acrobatic and fearless team member at the top of every pyramid and formation. The activity of the flyer is many, many times more dangerous than a football play. The incidence of concussion in flyers in cheerleading is more than tenfold what it is in football players. The same is true of the incidence of catastrophic injuries.

An injury to the flyer almost always is caused by a "collapsed pyramid" or an improperly executed dismount. Either somebody who was supposed to catch her out of the air fumbled the assignment, or she overshot her target. In either case, the flyer comes down hard. Frequently, the surface on which she's performing contributes to the problem. Cheer workouts and training often take place on soft, forgiving surfaces such as gym mats. Yet when squads are cheering in front of the crowds, that changes. Now they're doing stunts at a basketball pavilion on — it scares me just to say it out loud — hardwood floors, the world's worst surface for what's being attempted. Even synthetic tracks at football stadiums aren't appropriate for these activities. I can't imagine many things as risky as throwing someone twenty feet in the air with only a few sets of arms between her and a hardwood floor.

Adult leaders also need to be aware of the issue of fatigue. I know of a number of unfortunate cases in which cheerleaders were performing beyond their physical limits. They were tired. They were dehydrated. Their focus was off, and that probably contributed, in a major way, to the injury that happened. So, practice is good, but practice should be supervised. If kids are getting tired, they shouldn't be forced to do the "one more time" thing.

Mixed Martial Arts

Please don't interpret what I say here as an endorsement of mixed martial arts for kids. It's definitely not that. The last thing I want to encourage is kids, at any age, hitting somebody in the head. And not only the head. MMA is the only recognized sport I can think of in which you whack your opponent not only with fists and forearms but with elbows and knees — almost anywhere on your opponent's body. Almost anything is fair game.

In defense of MMA, I can say the following: Although children should not engage in the contact aspect of the sport until age fourteen at least, I see no problem with kids' learning proper techniques and fundamentals of the sport earlier. They can benefit from working on maneuvers, both offensive and defensive. As long as contact is taken out of the activity, I'm onboard.

The next point may seem odd coming from someone in the profession of protecting brains. But if your child is going to be involved in a *mano a mano* sport in which blows to the head are within the rules, MMA has advantages — minor, perhaps minuscule advantages, but still advantages. In MMA, the whole body is fair game. With a few exceptions, it's legal, even advisable, to pound your opponent from head to foot. Contrast that with boxing, in which the allowable target is half that area — blows below the waist aren't permitted. The result, I believe, is that the head takes significantly less trauma in most MMA bouts than in a boxing match. (As I said, I'm damning with faint praise.)

Another factor is the length of MMA bouts versus boxing matches. Because the pace is so frenetic, perhaps, MMA matches are much shorter, five rounds for a championship MMA event to twelve rounds for a championship boxing event.

Our interest here is children, and I have stated my strong recommendation that kids be banned from the hitting aspect of MMA until age fourteen. Until then, limit involvement of children to learning techniques. Any hitting to the head should wait even longer — I believe until age eighteen.

I say that simply because an eighteen-year-old is an adult making an informed decision about what he wants to do with his body. That gives him the right to deliver and receive blows to the head, if that's his choice. Before eighteen, the parents are deciding for a child who, in the eyes of the law, is still a child. I'm uncomfortable with parents determining whether it's okay for their kid to get their brain rattled. The kid may really want it and the kid may not want it. It's a decision to be made when we're consenting adults, not before. Adding to the complexity, children are impressionable. They tend to gravitate to the activities that their parents are passionate about. I've seen children who've grown up around boxing who were fighting by the age of eleven or twelve, though it's an activity that most kids would never volunteer for. Likewise, most of us wouldn't gravitate to driving at the Indianapolis 500. If your parents were racecar drivers, if you were riding go-carts fifty miles an hour by the time you were eight or nine, now it's a different story. The Indianapolis 500 doesn't seem so fast. I'm fine with allowing athletes to choose the risks they take with their brains. Let's wait until they're adults, however.

Skateboarding

There's a reason they're called action sports. To hop on a skateboard or zoom down a slope on a snowboard, you have to be a bit of a risk taker. Maybe even a thrill seeker.

Skateboarders typically do a reasonable job of looking out for their safety. Most are diligent about wearing helmets, a first line of defense against head trauma. Many are above-average athletes. They seem to have an innate sense of balance and ability for knowing where their bodies are in space. Skateboarders have an edge over snowboarders. In the event of trouble, they can easily separate from their boards. They're not lashed to their equipment.

There are dangers, of course. Skateboarders do fly off their boards at high speeds. The landing spots tend to be hard surfaces — in the street, asphalt; at skate parks, concrete. The way they fall also contributes to the concussion risk. Usually it's on their back with their head snapping back and colliding with something hard.

Research about skateboarding and head trauma is relatively scarce. Because it's not a scholastic sport — there aren't many middle school skateboard teams — relatively little research has been done in this area. We lack information about important things — whether skateboarding at a skate park is significantly safer than on the street. And we could know more about the protection offered by skateboard helmets.

My advice to parents is to get a good helmet. And if your kid has had some injuries, get him into another activity. Some may have inherent coordination issues. Others are inherent risk takers. There are kids who play it safe generally. Others are kamikazes and couldn't if they tried. If your kid's a kamikaze, find another sport.

Tennis

Any time you get out of bed, you're at risk of a concussion. Kids come into our office all the time with injuries from walking into ledges and slipping in bathtubs. The list goes on of injuries just as serious as anything that happens in a hockey game yet are total flukes.

Which brings us to tennis. Concussions in tennis are rare, but they are possible, and a child with complaints of a headache or nausea shouldn't be dismissed simply because she was playing a sport in which concussions "don't happen." Years ago, I witnessed a tennis concussion that is still fresh in my memory. I was playing doubles with three friends. A few points into the match, a situation arose much like in a baseball game when fielders converge on the pop fly — infielders going back, outfielders rushing in. In this case, one player came in a few steps, the other drifted back, and both took a big overhead stroke. If their rackets had collided, no one would have been hurt. Instead, the player behind swung through the ball and his racket came down and walloped his partner, striking him in the forehead. There was a groan. And then the player who'd taken the blow went down. He stayed down for a while as we tried to stop the bleeding. He had a nice laceration that required sutures. Of course, he also had a concussion.

Naming every non-collision sport in which kids can have concussions would add two dozen pages and at least that many sports to this chapter, starting with pole-vaulting, field hockey, snowboarding, and BMX biking. (Not that long ago, I treated a patient injured while playing Frisbee.) There probably isn't a sport played by children that is concussion-proof.

I can make my point simply with a reminder that whatever the sport, parents and coaches should assume nothing and should listen to the child.

4

Baseline Testing

I tell the kids that this test is designed to be a tool. We're doing this so we can give the doctors a tool to better treat our student-athletes when an injury happens in or out of school.

— JIM QUATROMONI, Hull High School athletic director (*Boston Globe*)

AT MANY HIGH SCHOOLS, sports seasons no longer begin in the gym or on the practice field. They start with a young athlete seated at a laptop computer. Before a youth player joins a team, she must submit to a test measuring the normal intellectual functioning of her brain. A few years ago, requiring a brain test would have been scoffed at. Few schools were using them.

Why test the brains of uninjured kids? How is the information mined from such tests helpful in the days and weeks after a concussion?

The computerized exams are a snapshot of how the brain functions when healthy — different tests for different regions of the brain. They serve as a reference point or, in the vernacular of concussion management, a baseline. If a young athlete sails through the season without an injury to the head, the test probably isn't referred to. An apt analogy might be a life insurance policy. As long as the insured person remains in good health, the policy stays locked in a file drawer. And if the child has a concussion? A physician with a background in treating concussions will have critical information with which to manage the injury.

Computerized testing is a highly visible example of technology being harnessed to prevent and manage head trauma in sports. It's also an industry on a steep growth curve. In a few years, an industry that previously did not exist has morphed into one generating tens of millions of dollars and encompassing an array of computerized tests. They have names such as Head Minder, Cogsport, ANAM, and the most widely used and commercially successful — ImPACT. The ImPACT test can be completed in twenty minutes and is given almost anywhere, though the location often is a school or physician's office. Test monitors include athletic trainers, school nurses, athletic directors, team doctors, and psychologists. Before giving the test to others, these professionals are often tested at least three times themselves so they're familiar with the ins and outs and can guide students confidently. ImPACT then tabulates the results in tables and charts and generates a neurocognitive profile so extensive that it covers six pages.

ImPACT comprises four parts. Part one covers demographics and health history — similar to filling out a personal medical background at the pediatrician's office. Part two asks the test taker for information about symptoms and other conditions related to previous concussions. These questions include the date of the test taker's most recent concussion (if any), the hours slept the previous night, and the names of prescription medicines he is currently taking. If the young athlete is experiencing concussion symptoms — twenty-two are listed — the symptoms and their severity are noted.

Part three — the true evaluation — is the neurocognitive test. This section consists of six "modules," or exercises designed to test different thinking parts of the brain.

"Word Discrimination" measures powers of attention and what's referred to as verbal recognition memory, which is the ability to recall verbal information. In this part, twelve words flash fleetingly on the screen. That list is followed by another list made up of a few words from the previous list mixed in with some different ones. The goal is to pick out those repeating words, no easy task considering how briefly the test subject got to see them.

In "Color Match," the test reaction time is being measured, along with impulse control and response inhibition. A color word appears on the screen in that same color (the word *blue* in the color blue). Other times, the word is presented in a different color (the word *blue* in the color red). The test subject responds as quickly as she can to what she sees, clicking "correct" when the color and the word correspond and "incorrect" when they don't.

Likewise, "Design Memory" evaluates visual memory and attention using shapes and designs (unlike "Word Discrimination," which tests the same only using words). "Xs and Os" is a test of visual memory and processing speed. "Symbol Match" looks at visual processing speed, learning, and memory, and "Three Letter Memory" grades memory and visual-motor response speed.

It's worth repeating that the purpose of baseline testing is to get a reading of normal brain function and capacity, not to identify the Einsteins among us. Most kids I have spoken to get this. They understand it's not a college entrance exam to be studied for or fretted over. Some even seem to enjoy the challenge involved in navigating memory tests and visual cues. Teenagers? Enjoying a test?

This is also a good place to insert a reminder about the limitations of ImPACT. As effective as it can be, it is a cognitive test only; it measures the brain's ability to think. It has nothing to do with the critical brain functions of balance and vision, which also can be adversely affected by head trauma. For that reason, ImPACT (and other tests measuring cognition only) should not be used as the one and only baseline exam.

The story of how ImPACT got its start is a lesson in entrepreneurship at its best and most improbable. The ImPACT program — the acronym stands for Immediate Post-concussion Assessment and Cognitive Testing — was started in the 1990s. Its founders are two respected scientists who then were working at the University of Pittsburgh: Mark Lovell, a PhD neuropsychologist, and Joseph Maroon, a neurosurgeon and Steelers neurosurgical consultant. Lovell traces the seed of the idea that became ImPACT to a concussion he suffered as a teenager. The experience sparked an interest in the science of the brain that grew in his college and graduate school years. While working on research at the University of Pittsburgh, he was pulled into a project to create a test that would measure the cognitive function of players on the Pittsburgh Steelers football team. Before the season, Steelers players were given an old-fashioned, non-computerized test, which served as a baseline. The test was repeated on players who had concussions during the season, and Lovell compared the results.

Lovell and Maroon continued work on the test, eventually developing a version for young athletes. Every year, their concept gains wider acceptance. Today, approximately two million kids have taken it, and ImPACT is now offered in fifteen languages, including Portuguese, Swedish, and Mandarin Chinese. The company has become so big and and profitable that recently Lovell gave up his academic appointments at the University of Pittsburgh to become ImPACT's full-time president.

Some of ImPACT's most impressive strides have been in the marketing realm, where against all odds it has turned a computerized brain function test into something cool and even sought-after by young athletes. A highly visible example of this image-making is the company's alliance with the national retailer Dick's Sporting Goods. In 2011, Dick's did something groundbreaking for a company with its reach and brand recognition. The big-box store created a national advertising campaign around a neuropsychological test. In TV advertisements, Dick's urged parents and coaches to have kids take a baseline test. Dick's hired Jerome Bettis, the bruising ex–football player known as "The Bus," to appear in a commercial. Bettis strolls down the aisle in a Dick's store, picks up a helmet, and says, "You wouldn't get on the field without this—and you shouldn't get on the field without a baseline concussion test either." As part of the campaign, Dick's promised to pay for testing of athletes at more than 3,300 schools. In all, Dick's helped more than one million young athletes receive ImPACT exams.

Like most cognitive tests, ImPACT is widely used as a baseline exam—that is, as an assessment of cognitive brain function before a concussion. The exam generates a score. The score is a measure of the full capacity of the brain when uninjured. Later, if the young athlete is hurt, she is tested again. The scores are compared and are used to help the doctor determine the extent of the impairment.

Similarly, the baseline exam is valuable in highlighting conditions that may affect scoring yet are unrelated to the patient's head trauma. Migraine headaches are an example. Attention deficit disorder (ADD), attention deficit hyperactivity disorder (ADHD), depression, anxiety disorders, and panic attacks also can affect performance on the test, skewing the results significantly.

A patient's recovery from concussion can differ depending on whether there is a baseline exam. The patient will recover with or without a baseline, because with very rare exceptions patients with concussions get better. But without a baseline, the path to recovery will have unexpected twists and turns.

Back in the 1980s, one of most promising quarterbacks in the National Football League was David Woodley. Woodley had all the physical attributes needed to be a star. He was big and strong. He had a powerful throwing arm. He was one of the most intelligent quarterbacks in the league. He was so intelligent, in fact, that his brain functioned as well with a concussion as the brains of many of us who have never suffered one.

Late in his career, Woodley was playing for the Pittsburgh Steelers. The Steelers were one of the dominant teams of that era. Still, their offensive line had occasional lapses. In a game early in the season, protection broke down. Woodley was sacked. He suffered a concussion. The diagnosis was made right away by the team doctors. Woodley sat out the rest of the game. The next week he still had symptoms, so he was out of that game too.

The Steelers asked him to take a then experimental test to measure his cognitive function — his thinking. The test would later be known as ImPACT.

Woodley agreed and scored well, solidly in the average range. Based on the result, the Steelers wanted Woodley to play. He wasn't sure he was ready. He still wasn't feeling himself. "You may say I'm fine. I know I'm not fine. I'm taking longer to figure things out than I would normally."

Woodley sat out again. The next week, the Steelers tested Woodley and this time his scores were much higher. Off the charts. In fact, his IQ was 138, genius level. So Woodley had been right. He had been impaired. With no baseline test, which few teams were using at the time, his scores appeared normal.

Years later, Doug Flutie reported a similar experience. Flutie had a long career in the pros in three leagues — the defunct U.S. Football League, the Canadian Football League, and the NFL. His most famous moment came when as a collegiate quarterback for Boston College he threw a famous Hail Mary touchdown pass to lift BC over the University of Miami. That year, he also won the Heisman Trophy as college football's top player.

Flutie was a daring, darting, scrambling quarterback. He tells about a time when, playing for San Diego in the NFL, he suffered a concussion. He said nothing about it. For the next few weeks, he continued playing, though not all that well. In those three games he threw something like eight interceptions. That was far from the normal Doug Flutie. He knew it and so did the Chargers' coaching staff. The concussion had dulled Flutie's ability to think and act quickly. It caused slow decisions and bad decisions. He shouldn't have been on the field. Had the Chargers' medical staff been able to compare before and after studies, he would have been on the sidelines.

Today baseline testing still isn't helping as many kids as it should. Thinking back on a recent week in my office, a typical one, I saw twelve patients with post-concussion syndrome. Almost all were young athletes injured while playing sports. Not one in the dozen had been given an ImPACT, Head Minder, or other baseline exam before his or her concussion. Without a baseline, managing a concussion is always difficult and always involves more guesswork on the part of the physician. It's simply more complicated to judge when the young athlete has returned to her "normal." In some patients, though, that complication is huge. A while back, a female athlete came to see me. She had been referred to my office from a doctor in Boston who'd been managing her post-concussion syndrome for many months. The previous spring, the young woman suffered a severe concussion. By June, she was somewhat better, and the following month, she had an ImPACT test for the first time. (It was not a baseline test, of course. A baseline occurs before a concussion.)

The test result was startling. The scores for verbal memory and reaction times were solidly in the average range, a good sign indicating that she was making progress. In contrast, her score for visual memory was extremely low, at the first percentile. This was off-the-charts low given that a score below the twenty-fifth percentile is considered grossly impaired.

The situation was a puzzle for the physician, the family, and especially the young woman. In nearly all ways, she was making a normal recovery, but one aspect of brain function was testing not just below average but well below average.

The doctor did the right thing, continuing to limit her activities until the next test, which everyone hoped and expected would show a rebound of that lagging score. But when the young woman was tested again in August, her visual memory advanced from the first percentile to the second — a negligible improvement at best.

At that point, the young woman and her parents made the decision to see me. It had been months since the concussion, and the symptoms had completely gone away. Yet each time she took the ImPACT test, the score in visual memory was very low. As her doctor, I couldn't be sure whether the part of the brain controlling that function was still injured and needed more rest or her visual memory deficits preceded the concussion and were unrelated. The point of this story, and others like it, is that when there is a baseline test, there are fewer questions, and the ones that remain are easier to address. The young woman in this case was held out of sports for many months, and other activities were restricted too. It was good, cautionary medicine. Yet much of the layoff might have been unnecessary.

Even with all the progress in recent years, baseline testing has yet to become the norm in youth sports. Many more athletes be-gin a sports season without a baseline than with one. One reason is the design of these exams, many of which are tailored for teens and older athletes. ImPACT is typical in that it is not given to children until the age of twelve. By then, some kids have been playing tackle football — not to mention falling out of trees and off skate-boards — for half their lives. Clearly, baselines for much younger children are needed.

Such tests finally are being developed. As I write this, ImPACT is rolling out a version of its exam that is recommended for children starting at the age of five. It gathers similar data about memory and reaction time, according to the lead investigator for the project, Dr. Gerry Gioia, chief of Pediatric Neuropsychology at the Children's National Medical Center in Washington, D.C. But the test accom-plishes this in a *Sesame Street*–style format. The "Xs and Os" test in the standard exam becomes "Wacky Tacky Tic Tac Toe," and "Color Match" turns into "Funny Fruits and Vegetables." In that one, kids decide whether the picture of the fruit or vegetable they are being shown is in the correct color. Click yes for a yellow banana, no for a black carrot, and so on.

It takes more than one type of test to compile a comprehensive baseline. ImPACT measures cognition, the thinking and reasoning parts of the brain. This includes the medial temporal lobe and fron-tal lobe connections and capacities such as memory, concentration, attention, executive function, and multitasking. But concussions also may cause trauma to the calcarine cortex, which is in the back of the brain and controls vision, and the cerebellum, at the top of the neck, where balance and coordination are regulated. ImPACT and other cognitive testing wouldn't establish a baseline or reveal deficits in these areas of the brain; more and different evaluations are needed.

An option that more youth organizations should consider is the King-Devick Test. Unlike Head Minder and ImPACT, King-Devick is not a cognitive or neuropsychological test. Nor is it a sit-at-your-laptop-and-recall-words-on-a-list test. Instead, King-Devick measures what are referred to as saccadic eye movements, tracking the ways our eyes respond to various prompts and commands. Post-concussion symptoms can slow those movements considerably.

Some feel that this sort of exam is a better way to gauge the overall effects of a concussion than a neuropsychological exam. Eye movements have connections to multiple parts of the brain — they're not limited to the "vision part." So a King-Devick exam will reveal deficits in any or all of them. It's the difference between taking a test covering U.S. history versus one on world history.

The entrepreneurs behind King-Devick promote the test as a simple and economical alternative to ImPACT. The only equipment needed is a stopwatch. It can be given on a pool deck or a softball diamond — anywhere. Nearly anyone can be trained as a test monitor. These factors make King-Devick a good fit for youth sports programs, or so say its backers. I agree. However, it's one test and one picture of a young athlete's brain. A complete baseline exam requires more than one type of exam. And similarly, if a child has had a concussion, one test is not enough to assess the situation fully. The child should have a more thorough workup — including the physician inquiring about conditions that affect concussion recovery, past concussion history, a symptom checklist, and a complete neurological exam including detailed balance testing.

Baseline testing is beneficial for many reasons, none more important than its value in helping to avoid two bad outcomes: one, that your injured child will be cleared to return to sports too soon; two, that your healthy child will be held out of sports or school for weeks after she could have safely gone back. It's inexpensive, painless, and easy to do. There aren't any good reasons not to have your child take one, or none that I can think of. Like all good things, however, a baseline exam can be turned inside out. We know, for example, that the test can be manipulated by a test taker.

The manipulators sometimes are professional athletes. Peyton Manning is unquestionably one of the top quarterbacks in the history of National Football League. His career statistics certainly prove he deserves to be in the conversation. Yet Manning is among the pro athletes who have acknowledged that they deliberately scored poorly on baseline tests. "After a concussion, you take the same test, and if you do worse than you did on the first test, you can't play. So I just try to do badly on the first test," he told ESPN.com in 2011. Manning took quite a bit a criticism for those remarks and a few days later backtracked, saying he'd never deliberately tanked a test. In the earlier interview, he explained, he'd just been having some fun. "I understand the seriousness of concussions," he told the *Indianapolis Star*. I'm not in a position to say whether Manning was kidding or quite serious. Either way, it isn't my idea of a great joke.

Baseline testing also can be used in questionable ways by physicians. In some clinics, if a young athlete comes in with concussion symptoms, one of the first things done is a neuropsychological test. The thinking is reasonable as far as it goes: The sooner the patient's status is assessed, the better. As time goes by, and the brain recovers, the score should improve.

What this approach ignores is that while the patient is symptomatic, the test itself may make the person worse. Taking it does, after all, cause cognitive stress. Stress is precisely what we counsel our patients to avoid. I just can't agree with doing something *for* the patient that has the effect of doing something *to* the patient. For that reason, I do not give neuropsychological tests to my patients while they are symptomatic.

Testing an injured athlete over and over during his recovery from a concussion is also common in some medical practices. There is a test two weeks after the concussion, then six weeks, then three months, and so on. I do not agree with this practice either. There are several reasons that it's done, and I am passing them on here so that you can discuss them with your child's doctor if needed. One reason is for the parents of the injured child. The test serves as a yardstick. It results in a score, which can be compared to the score on the next test. In that way, parents can be reassured that their child is improving. In effect, the test makes it easier for the physician to say to Mom and Dad, "See the score? He's not back to baseline but he's getting better." The approach ignores a significant point — taking the test over and over may be slowing the recovery of the young athlete.

Repeat testing can have another negative and unintended effect. After several repetitions, it's possible for some children to memorize the test. That is, as they take it over and over it becomes second nature to them, so they can anticipate better what part of the test is up next and perhaps score higher than they would have otherwise.

Of course, another reason that young athletes may be getting tested more often than really is necessary is that every time a doctor gives the test, there's a fee to the patient or the insurance company. The doctor can bill for it. Not a lot of physicians run their practices that way. But some do, and that's important to acknowledge.

Privacy concerns also factor into the opinions of some about neuropsychological testing. Some parents are troubled that their children are required to submit to a baseline test before being cleared to play school sports. They have concerns that the test results might not remain confidential. Not long ago, I read about a child on a high school swim team who was required to take the test before starting her sports season. Many school districts in Oregon and Washington State do not let students on the field (or in the pool) before they have had a screening. The father of the young lady was concerned to say the least. He was quoted as saying, "That really sent shivers up my spine. I was being challenged. That's what it felt like more than anything else, that my parental authority and my decision-making were being challenged."

I share concerns about privacy, and I understand a parent's strong feelings about choosing what's best for a child without interference from school. Yet those concerns should not be obstacles to safety in sports. For me, the benefit to a child from a baseline test far outweighs the intrusiveness of being required to take one.

In fact, baseline testing should be expanded. A cognitive exam should be accompanied by a balance test (feet side by side, one foot heel to toe in front of the other, and more). Anything that will be tested after a concussion should be tested before — a lesson learned from the imperfect diagnosis of the former NFL quarterback David Woodley. These various baselines rarely are available to me when I see young athletes.

Testing is one example of technology changing youth sports and making it safer, but there are other technological developments that parents and coaches should learn about. Axial accelerometers, small sensors that measure forces generated by blows to the head, are being attached to helmets. The information is captured in real time — each helmet crack as it happens — and can be sent to a laptop on the sidelines. The company that has been in front in developing this technology is Simbex, a New Hampshire–based firm that has backed extensive research into hits and helmets. A few years ago, a Brown University scientist used Simbex to analyze hits absorbed by football players at Brown, Dartmouth, and Virginia Tech. The study in the *Journal of Biomechanics* isolated head trauma by the positions on the team and reported these findings: The most forceful hits to the head were taken by running backs and quarterbacks, and linemen and linebackers took more head blows than players at any other position. During the three seasons covered by the study, Simbex documented 286,636 head blows to 314 players. Many players received more than 1,000 head hits exceeding 20 g's in a season.

This research and more like it is changing football. There's a great need for limiting exposure to the blows that are a part of the sport at all levels. To that end, a device currently in development holds much promise. It's a small sensor worn on a headband inside the helmet. It's as portable as a sweatband or do-rag. At the end of the football season, the band moves to the next sport's activity with the athlete and can be worn with a bike helmet, lacrosse helmet, and an ice hockey helmet.

Versatility is key, because for the technology to catch on it must be affordable. Schools already short on funds don't have budgets to purchase sensors for every helmet in the equipment room.

Eventually, sensors inside helmets will open up a whole new understanding of head trauma. They will give us the capability to track all forces to the head, the big wallops and the small subconcussive blows routinely absorbed by players in collision sports. From research studies already completed, we know some high school athletes are taking more than a thousand subconcussive blows in a football season. What we can't know yet is the effects these blows have on young players — now and years from now. No head trauma is good head trauma. But is a childhood spent being pounded and whiplashed in ice hockey and tackle football truly damaging?

As I am writing this book, experts in sports concussion are coming together to discuss how to set head trauma thresholds — in a game, a week, and a season. We've never tried to do this before, never circled a precise number and agreed that after a certain point the hitting has to stop.

What needs to happen with brain injury is similar to what already is happening with elbow and shoulder injuries in youth baseball. For years — decades, really — organized youth baseball did little to protect kid pitchers from overusing their throwing arms. In the last few years, as studies have established a connection between pitchers who throw too many innings and play too many months and an alarming spike in arm injuries, organizations such as Little League Baseball have stepped in with mandatory pitch counts. A child is permitted to toss only so many pitches in a game and in the course of a week. The numbers fall on a sliding scale that changes with the child's age. Football or ice hockey "hit counts" could function similarly. Limits would be based on the best scientific evidence available and be modified as more is learned.

We're gearing up to put these ideas into action. In February 2012, the Sports Legacy Institute released a white paper proposing that leading experts convene to discuss a process for developing standards. As cofounders of SLI, Chris Nowinski and I are committed not just to talking about hit counts but to seeing that they are implemented at all levels of youth sports. Eventually, we expect guidelines will address the minimum threshold for a hit, maximum hits per day, week, season, and year (stratified by age), and a minimum number of rest days for players who reach limits in any of these categories. It's too soon to predict where lines will be drawn, but clearly hit counts at youth levels will be lower than for high school, and they in turn will be lower than for colleges. In other words, when formulating hit counts, age and physical maturity matter. It is also probable that we will start with hit counts per season and address the number per day and year as more and better science becomes available.

The technology, remarkable though it is, may be fallible in recording the precise linear and rotational accelerations. There are biomechanists who believe Simbex does an excellent job measuring hits that go through the center of gravity of the head (e.g., a hit right through the ear hole of the helmet or squarely in the middle of your forehead) but is not precisely accurate in measurement of hits off the center of gravity. A hit that primarily swivels the neck and head may be inaccurately recorded by Simbex. So would blows caused by most headers in soccer, spills in volleyball, and headfirst slides in baseball. Currently, biomechanists funded independently by the NFL and by the National Operating Committee on Standards for Athletic Equipment are studying the accuracy of off-center hits as recorded by the Simbex system. Still, concern over the limitations does not lessen the value of the system in recording the number of hits, which is our major focus.

Have you heard about the miraculous headband for youth soccer? It's one of many anti-concussion products billed as using the "latest technology." Don't be taken in. Most of these gadgets are worthless.

Soccer headbands are a notorious rip-off. They don't reduce brain trauma or reduce anything else that justifies the price. Headbands *may* reduce the chance of sustaining a scalp laceration. They are good-looking and are worn by some players as a fashion statement. Despite the claims made by entrepreneurs behind them, they are not protection against head trauma.

This claim itself is dangerous. Players wearing these products may play more aggressively, believing they have a force field around them. In reality, they have a padded band.

Certain chin straps concern me for the same reasons. The companies behind some of the widely advertised products cannot possibly deliver on the promises they make. One that gets a lot of press has an axial accelerometer built into the part that rests on the player's chin when it's snapped in place. On the accelerometer are colored lights, one red, one green. When a player takes a hit, lights flash to alert the player and his coach that the impact was minor and the player is safe (green light) or that the impact was severe and he ought to come out of the game for an evaluation (red light). Do not buy the stop-and-go chin strap. To think that a kid with concussion symptoms might not be evaluated because a light bulb failed to turn red is disturbing and dangerous.

Likewise, I'm not impressed with the celebrity spokesmen who stand behind some of these supposed anti-concussion aids. The chin strap is endorsed by the star NFL defensive lineman Ndamukong Suh. Suh is an outstanding tackle for the Detroit Lions, one of the best in the NFL. The company's ads suggest that in addition to Suh, four or five NFL players wear the chin straps. All that celebrity power should not obscure this point: There isn't an ounce of science behind the claims.

Parents and coaches are vulnerable, willing to spend freely to keep their kids safe in sports, yet wary of being taken advantage of. Before buying a miracle chin strap or a magical nutritional supplement, do your own research. Check reputable sources on the Internet. E-mail or call a physician with expertise in treating head trauma. Describe the product and ask, "Is this worth $79.99?" You'll get an informed, unbiased answer, and it's likely to be no.

5

Post-Concussion Syndrome and Second Impact Syndrome

> While all my classmates were involved in senior activities,
> I was home depressed and in constant pain, and life had become
> a blur. Every day I endure memory loss, lack of concentration,
> depression, slow processing speed and cognitive effects that
> make my everyday life a battle.
>
> — MICHELLE PELTON, a high school athlete from Massachusetts
> (*New York Times*)

> In my gut, I should have told someone, but I didn't.
> I didn't want to come off like a sissy.
>
> — KEVIN SAUM, West Morris High School football player. He can
> never play collision sports again. (*Gloucester County* [New Jersey] *Times*)

IT STARTED WITH A bump on the head. It seemed harmless. Rose-Marie Fuchs was playing volleyball with her club team, facing the net and preparing to return the serve. The next thing she remembers was the thwack of the volleyball on the back of her head. "She didn't cry. She was just stunned," recalls her mother, Ann-Marie.

Rose-Marie stayed in the game to the finish, but when she got home she didn't feel well. She was sapped of energy and complained that her head hurt. Her parents wondered whether she had a strep infection that several kids at school were recovering from. It seemed like a logical explanation for the symptoms.

Except that Rose-Marie didn't improve. After several weeks of watching their daughter struggle with headaches, nausea, and an uncharacteristically short temper, her parents became concerned.

Rose-Marie Fuchs

They took her to their family doctor and learned that she did not have mononucleosis or Lyme disease. Confident that the symptoms were about to lift, Ann-Marie encouraged her daughter to keep going. Rose-Marie went to school and continued to show up for volleyball.

"I'd force her to play," she tells me. "And every time she'd play, she was sick again."

In the next three months, Rose-Marie was examined by an infectious disease specialist and a pediatric neurologist. The Fuchses also continued to consult with their family doctor. "No one came up with anything," Ann-Marie recalls.

Many days, Rose-Marie didn't have the strength to go to school. When she did, she often was home before dismissal, complaining of fatigue and "vise-gripping headaches." She spoke of "feeling dumb" and "being in a haze" in class.

Four months after her volleyball accident, Rose-Marie was diagnosed with post-concussion syndrome. Her mom comments that it wasn't diagnosed as much as revealed — all the other possibilities had been ruled out. Frustrated and nearly out of ideas, Ann-Marie sat down at her computer and searched "volleyball and concussion." She learned that there was help for her daughter. "I felt like I was getting a medical degree on the Web."

Rose-Marie and her mom came to my office about three weeks after the diagnosis. That first visit, she had more than a dozen symptoms of concussion, a severe case. Yet mother and daughter were relieved to learn that with rest, her brain would heal.

Post-concussion syndrome is a name given to concussions that last an unusually long time and challenge patients with unusually intense symptoms. Most concussions resolve in seven to ten days and athletes return to their normal activities in two weeks. Approximately 20 percent are post-concussion syndrome cases. (In my practice, the percentage is 50 percent.) Symptoms last at least a month and can persist much longer. There isn't an upper limit, and I have seen athletes who after several years still hadn't shaken every symptom.

Rest is the most effective therapy for post-concussion syndrome — physical and cognitive rest. A patient with PCS should limit strenuous activity. Sports have to stop completely. When symptoms are gone, the patient is cleared to begin working out again, in small increments, then more actively if the symptoms do not return. Thus, the hockey superstar Sidney Crosby of the Pittsburgh Penguins was able to begin skating after a long layoff when his symptoms cleared, and stopped when those symptoms returned some weeks later. He could try again when he was symptom-free.

Resting the brain is problematic. We can't rest our brains completely, even when we're sleeping or watching Snooki on *Jersey Shore*. In a post-concussion syndrome patient, the goal is to virtually eliminate activities that are intellectually stimulating, as well as situations that could exacerbate symptoms. As mentioned in a previous chapter, these restrictions really shrink the normal social and school life of a child. We recommend that our patients avoid places that are busy, noisy, or bright, and where they might encounter crowds.

That rules out shopping malls, sporting events, movie theaters, and political rallies, for example. Often after a concussion, kids continue watching TV without restriction. No one tells them not to. And it seems perfectly safe. It's happening at home in a quiet room. Yet the stimulation from staring at the screen can cause a setback.

School can be an especially hostile place, as Rose-Marie Fuchs discovered. Many of the starred items on the Avoid list are unavoidable in high school — loud halls, brightly lit classrooms, chaos in the cafeteria, exams to study for and stress over. Exposure to one or two has potential to prolong post-concussion syndrome. After her volleyball concussion, Rose-Marie struggled to keep up. In her condition, it wasn't possible. She missed thirty days of classes. The days she was able to make it to school, she was washed out, exhausted.

School officials and teachers are becoming more supportive of concussion patients. Years ago, a student telling his teacher that he had a concussion and needed more time to take an exam would have gotten a sideways glance. That doesn't happen as frequently now. Cooperation between schools and the physician has improved markedly. Physicians realize they absolutely must have a partnership with the schools and have gotten smarter about how to communicate. Here's one example: When young patients see me, they receive a letter for a school nurse or teacher. At the top is my name, office address, and phone number — so that finding me to discuss the condition of a patient is easy. At the bottom is my signature. The body of the letter outlines restrictions that I am placing on the child's activity. Here are my five standard rules:

1. She should not be asked to take more than one examination a day, she may require additional time to take examinations, and she should not be given lengthy homework.
2. She should do no physical activities beyond light walking. She should not be doing gym or any sports, heavy lifting, physical exertion, or any activity with significant risk of falling or head trauma.
3. She should avoid unnecessary mental activity and espe-

cially refrain from video games, text messaging, e-mail, and other physical or cognitive intellectual activities that may provoke her post-concussion symptoms.

4. She should avoid any other stimulus or activity that causes any of her post-concussion symptoms to return or worsen.
5. No gym class for the time being. She should instead use that time for rest and/or study.

The letter is for academic teachers, nurses, and gym teachers. I recommend also sharing the same information — if not the letter itself — with the athlete's peers. Friends are an important source of support. They can help get their injured buddy through a tough time just by visiting him at home, sending occasional texts (not too many, though), and simply being around to listen. The peers are not as likely to stay in the picture if there's an information blackout. Because they are friends and are concerned, they'll have questions: *What's wrong? How did this happen? When will you be better? Are you really that sick?* These can be tough for a young person with post-concussion syndrome, but Rose-Marie tried to answer her friends. "Usually I said, 'I may look fine on the outside. I feel horrible inside.'"

Post-concussion syndrome patients eventually recover — almost every one. I'm not certain that all patients believe me when I tell them that they will. Regardless of how severe the symptoms are, I have no doubt they will get better. I think back to a young boy I treated whose memory was shot so totally that he'd forgotten how to do simple math problems. It took more than a year, but he recovered.

Because post-concussion syndrome patients are ill for months, symptoms can become intolerable. Someone who can't fall asleep and can't stay asleep not only has post-concussion syndrome but a miserable quality of life that plunges them into despair.

Sleep issues are especially troubling. They can lead to depression and other symptoms, making the situation far worse. I've treated patients so distraught that they told me, sobbing, "I want to end it" and

"I'm going to kill myself." We take those statements very seriously. A suicidal patient isn't permitted to go home until they have been evaluated by a psychiatrist.

Head trauma and thoughts of suicide are subjects that aren't discussed as often or openly as they should be, but they are truly important for parents, teachers, and coaches to understand. Fortunately, courageous people such as Matt Glass are speaking up. Matt suffered a concussion playing high school football and continued playing. Six weeks later, a second head injury left him no choice but to seek help for severe concussion symptoms. For more than a year, Matt struggled to hold on to his old life. At each step he seemed to be losing ground. He missed more than three months in a single school year. Twice he returned to classes only to pass out in front of classmates and teachers. Once, a fire alarm sounded and he fainted.

Nearly a year after the concussion, Matt hit bottom. On a Tuesday night, he drove the family car to Boston to get his computer fixed and didn't come home. His parents phoned the local police department to report him missing. He was finally reunited with his parents Thursday night. When police found Matt, he was confused and disoriented.

Matt's disappearance was the culmination of a hellish year. He'd been worn down by his unrelenting symptoms, which included headaches and severe sleep difficulties. At about that time, Matt became my patient. When we spoke in my office, I asked about his disappearance and why it had happened. "A lot of it was caused by stress and anxiety. I was anxious all the time," he said. "So many things raced through my mind. I wasn't sleeping well. I wasn't able to concentrate in school. I was dealing with depression.

"The whole time I was away I wasn't thinking that people were looking for me. My first thought when I snapped out of it was, 'What just happened?'"

Matt credits visits to a psychologist, which began after the incident, with speeding his recovery. For the first time, he was able to share his deepest and darkest fears. "If you're having suicidal thoughts after a concussion, chances are you're not talking about it," he said. "No one understood how it felt to have everything taken away — football, academic intelligence, even the way I felt and acted."

For patients who are struggling, I sometimes prescribe drugs. They are never a first option, however. There are many reasons to approach these medications with caution, including this important one: Drugs have desired effects and undesired ones, too. A drug that helps a patient doze and therefore is valuable may exacerbate other symptoms such as trouble concentrating or a feeling of being in a fog. In effect, making the patient better may also be making her worse. Then there's the reality about drug therapies: They can't heal the brain faster or better. In limited circumstances, though, they can bring relief to a patient while her brain heals.

Having said that I view prescription medications as a last resort, I would be remiss not to add that I prescribe medication in cases that fail to respond to physical and cognitive rest alone. This is especially true when one symptom dominates all other symptoms. For difficult cognitive or thought symptoms (feeling in a fog) or problems with concentration or memory, the neurostimulants in the methylphenidate group — Ritalin, Adderall, Concerta, Strattera, and Amantadine — can be very beneficial. For somatic symptoms such as headache, Amitriptyline, Nortriptyline, Propranolol, or Verapamil can help greatly. Trouble falling asleep can be helped by the prescription meds Trazodone or Ambien, and emotional difficulties may benefit from Lexapro or Zoloft. The doses of these medications are beyond the scope of this book, but in every case they are a process of trial and error, starting with the lowest dose that produces no side effects yet achieves the desired effect.

Other non-medicinal therapies that are employed with success in post-concussion syndrome include vestibular therapy (head and eye exercises) if dizziness or balance are primary symptoms, cognitive therapy for thought problems, and upper cervical spine physical therapy for pain in the upper neck and back of the head.

Before prescribing a drug, I ask post-concussion syndrome patients to consider other options. One of my recommendations is melatonin, a naturally occurring substance made by the brain. It can be purchased at a drugstore or a health food store without a prescription, and it's cheap — under nine dollars for a bottle of 120 capsules. Some patients have great results with melatonin and get back to something like their old sleep patterns.

People want to stick with what they know, and often my patients don't know much about yoga. I encourage them to try anyway. Yoga is great for improving flexibility and core strength, of course. Many concussion patients have difficulty with heightened anxiety, and for them yoga also can have a good effect. This isn't the place for a lengthy description of yoga, but suffice it to say that most people leave a yoga class feeling a lot less stressed than when they entered.

Recently, a highly successful businessman from the Boston area came to see me for his post-concussion syndrome. The first thing he did was tell me about a small dispute he'd had with his wife. He'd gone out to pick up curtain rods that she had ordered. When he got home, he installed the hardware and was feeling proud that he'd gotten that far with the project when his wife walked in and said, "Aren't you going to hang the curtains?"

He blew up. And the way he blew up clearly worried him. "That's not me," he said with regret in his voice.

When he finished telling his story, I said, "Don't blame yourself," and explained that concussions can increase anxiety and interfere with impulse control. "It probably couldn't have been helped."

Then I added, "Why not call a yoga studio?"

My patients who have taken classes didn't become Zen masters. Some only attended a few times. But they reported back that they were glad they'd tried it, and the same goes for the patients who have gotten into meditation, biofeedback, and several natural approaches to stress reduction.

Post-concussion syndrome patients often have had concussions that weren't managed properly. Their brains are exposed to a second injury and the situation becomes much worse than it was or needed to be. It's not the fault of the parent, coach, or player with the head injury, necessarily. This book isn't about blame. Things happen, and we deal with them with the knowledge we have at the time. Hearing about these young patients can only help other families.

Consider the story of Kayla DiBiasie. Kayla is a talented athlete who tried many sports and excelled at all. She was an avid snow skier (until a skiing concussion) and has played on high school teams in field hockey and her favorite sport, softball. Several years ago, Kayla was playing first base on her softball team and was slammed by a runner as she reached for an errant throw. She left the game and had a thorough medical workup — all the right steps. Still, she developed post-concussion syndrome.

"For a while after my concussion I had anxiety attacks. I would get really emotional over everything, big things and small things. I didn't know why," Kayla recalls. "That made me more anxious. If I was going to school and didn't know what to expect, that made me anxious. If I was going out somewhere and wasn't sure who would

Kayla DiBiasie

be there, that made me anxious. I kept reminding myself, *This is going to change. This won't go on forever. I have to take care of myself.*"

After doing all the right things, why did Kayla have such a difficult time recovering from her concussion? There was more to her story. This concussion was not Kayla's first. It was her third in twenty months. Concussions two and three happened six months apart. Concussions that are bunched that closely often are harder for the brain to overcome and the healing takes longer.

Susan DiBiasie, Kayla's mom, has another theory about Kayla's post-concussion syndrome, and I believe it also has merit. Kayla's first concussion occurred in field hockey. During a game, a ball bounced off a stick into the air and slammed Kayla's head, knocking her down. She was unconscious for fifteen seconds and left the game, but she came back and played until the end. That night, Kayla developed a headache that lasted for several days. She was not evaluated for a concussion.

Susan has regrets about everything that happened after Kayla hit the ground. "I remember that night Kayla telling me she had a headache, feeling nervous and asking myself, *Should I do something?*" she tells me. "I didn't want to make a mountain out of it and I was unsure how to proceed.

"I was totally ignorant of concussions. I didn't know enough to know what to do. If I could go back in time, I would not let her continue to play field hockey that day and I would get her to a doctor. I firmly believe if we'd handled the first one correctly, the subsequent ones would not have been so bad."

Chris Vanesian and Dylan Mello also wish they could go back in time. Chris, a soccer and basketball player, had post-concussion syndrome that wiped out much of his senior year of high school sports. Dylan, an ice hockey and soccer player, never even had any part of a senior season. By his senior year, he was sidelined from having had three concussions in ten months.

Both Dylan and Chris had concussions, and both went back to their teams before their symptoms cleared.

Neither would make the same choice again.

Chris was a senior captain on his basketball team. Around mid-season, while playing in a game, he took a charge and crashed his head against the floor. He came back two weeks later after persuading his coach and his mother that his symptoms had cleared. In the very first practice, he took a shot to the head from a teammate's elbow and knew that he had made a mistake. A few weeks later, he came to my office with seven concussion symptoms. I gave Chris my assessment. If he had another concussion (this was his third), the consequences might be even more serious. His symptoms lasted eighteen months.

"I could have missed a week. Instead I missed a year and a half," he tells me. "The lesson I learned is that I'm not invincible like most eighteen-year-olds think they are."

Dylan had the same teenage fearlessness, coupled with a strong sense that his coaches and teammates needed him. In one terrible

Chris Vanesian

year, he had three concussions. His mistake was rushing back from concussion number two. Three months after coming back to his high school soccer team with symptoms, he got hit in the head again. Even then Dylan continued to play for a few weeks before admitting to coaches and parents the agony he was in. "I was a sixteen-year-old ignorant kid who wanted to play sports no matter what," he says.

Dylan was an honor roll student accustomed to studying hard and excelling at school. That part of his life suddenly was upside down. When he tried to focus on a lecture or studied for an exam, his symptoms flared. He recalls a particularly bad experience with the SAT college entrance exam. After taking the exam, he had a severe dizzy spell that persisted for two days.

Dylan completed his senior year, but the effort exhausted him. We decided that the best course was to take an extended break from school and focus on getting well. For the next twelve months, Dylan's world shrank. He quit a part-time job, didn't go out with friends, eliminated heavy reading, and limited TV to two hours a day. Most mornings he slept until ten thirty. He was in bed by ten at night. His only activities were taking care of his dog and going to a local gym, where he was permitted to go through very light workouts. "I shut down everything," he recalled. "It was awful."

Rest was the best therapy. The headaches weren't paralyzing anymore. Dylan's other symptoms began to fade. He applied to Providence College and was accepted. When I spoke with Dylan not long ago, he was feeling better, though not back to his old self. "There's tightness around my eyes. I still have numbness in my feet. It's been so long since I've felt normal, I'm not sure I would know what normal is."

At least the mistakes of kids who play through serious injuries can be understood. After all, they're kids, and their inexperience and exuberance lead them astray. When grownups — coaches, in particular — make the same mistakes, it is difficult to explain.

Mirela Caron is a young gymnast who started in her sport at age three. In high school she was training twenty hours a week and doing quite well, even competing at the national level. At school one day, Mirela was doing bench presses during gym class when the bar slipped from her hands and a ninety-pound weight came down on her forehead. The accident caused a concussion, and Mirela had to put her training on hold as her brain healed and her symptoms faded. After two months she was symptom-free and cleared to begin light exercise. The workouts began that way, but in a short time Mirela's gymnastics coaches turned up the intensity beyond what had been recommended. Her symptoms came back, and what seemed like the final stages of her recovery turned into yet another long layoff.

"Coaches have their own versions of what's okay and what isn't," Sheree, Mirela's mom, told me. "At first, her workouts were just stretching. By the second week, she was being pushed and her heart rate was up, blood pressure was up, all those factors that cause exacerbation. The coach wanted what was best for her. But he didn't get it."

As disastrous as post-concussion syndrome is for young people, eventually the ordeal passes and they do recover. Many are able to go

Mirela Caron

back to competitive sports and some even to bruising collision sports such as football or ice hockey. Victims of second impact syndrome rarely get a second chance. Jaquan Waller, a young football player, is a tragic example. Jaquan was a star running back for Greenville Rose High School in North Carolina. In 2008, he left the field after what seemed an unremarkable carry and tackle. Suddenly, Jaquan collapsed on the sidelines. The next morning he died. The medical examiner cited second impact syndrome as the cause of death. Like other victims of second impact syndrome, Jaquan had been playing with a brain injury. Two days before the game in which he died, he had taken a big hit in a practice and suffered a mild concussion.

What is second impact syndrome? Our brains normally maintain a constant blood flow through a process called autoregulation. When the blood pressure rises in our brain, this causes a restriction in arterioles, small blood vessels that branch out from larger arteries. When blood pressure falls, the opposite occurs. Arterioles dilate, or relax, to maintain constant blood flow.

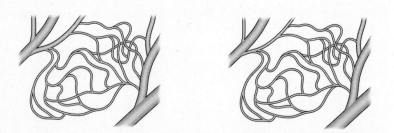

Baseline *(left)*: When blood pressure is normal, brain arteriole blood vessels are neither constricted nor dilated. **Increased blood pressure** *(right)*: The brain seeks to maintain a constant blood flow. The brain arteriole blood vessels constrict.

Second impact syndrome disrupts autoregulation. Blood pressure is normal or elevated, but when arterioles should be constricting, they're relaxed; blood rushes through them. The result is highly dangerous — a rapid and massive inflow of blood to the brain and an equally dramatic increase in the pressure inside the skull. It's a grave situation and often leads to herniation of the brain and death. The patients who survive are almost always severely disabled.

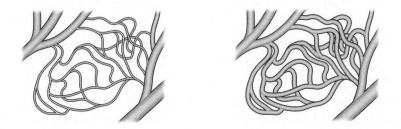

Decreased blood pressure *(left)*: As pressure falls, brain arteriole dilation occurs. Blood flow to the brain remains unchanged. **Dysautoregulation, or second impact syndrome** *(right)*: A serious disruption occurs. The brain acts as if blood pressure is low when it is not low; it's normal or may be elevated. Brain arteriole blood vessels dilate and blood rushes into the brain. A massive rise in intracranial pressure results. Within minutes, the brain can herniate, resulting in coma.

Each year, a few athletes lose their lives to second impact syndrome. How many is unclear. Since 1987 I have been involved in a research study that tracks catastrophic injuries causing death or permanent brain or spinal cord damage among high school and college football players in the United States. During a thirteen-year interval, the research team found ninety-four. Almost all were high school athletes. Nearly three quarters involved players who'd had a previous concussion that season. Approximately 40 percent were on the field despite having concussion symptoms at the time.

Ninety-four deaths in thirteen years aren't overwhelming considering that 1.1 million young people played high school football in 2009 alone. Yet many of those ninety-four deaths were preventable.

I've never treated a young athlete who died from second impact syndrome, a statement I hope I can make for the rest of my career. Because it is usually fatal, second impact syndrome ripples through a community, touching and darkening the lives of many. The injured player loses his life and his family deals with the questions and the grief. The other players on the field are also affected, left to wonder whether they made the tackle or threw the block that caused someone to die. Every one of these deaths could be avoided. Not all players recognize that. Often, neither do coaches and parents.

With a greater commitment to keeping players with head trauma symptoms off the field, deaths from second impact syndrome would go from a few to none.

Will Benson died of second impact syndrome in 2002. He was a fine student and the quarterback for St. Stephen's Episcopal School in Austin, Texas. In the first game of the season Will was in charge of the St. Stephen's offense, had the ball tucked under his arm, and was smacked down with a helmet-to-helmet hit. Will got up, got back to the huddle, and played the rest of the game. Several days later, Will acknowledged that he'd been coping with severe headaches. So he sat out the next game, another loss. He couldn't bear the thought of missing another game, so the following week, two weeks after the initial injury, Will was back in the St. Stephen's lineup, thinking not as much about his brain as the team's winless record.

In the first half, Will suddenly removed his helmet and walked off the field. He told his coach that he saw "big blobs." In the locker room a few minutes later, he lost consciousness. Five days after that, Will died from second impact syndrome. He was seventeen years old.

Will's death started a concussion awareness movement in Texas, led by Dick Benson, Will's dad. Dick Benson tirelessly lobbied the Texas legislature for a law to strengthen education about head trauma in youth sports. Those efforts paid off in 2007. The Texas legislature signed into law "Will's Bill," which requires athletic trainers and high school coaches to have concussion education, to be trained in CPR, and to know where to call for emergency help.

A terrible accident involving a thirteen-year-old football player from a community near Seattle, Washington, has taken things to the next level. In 2006, Zackery Lystedt, a star linebacker on his middle school football team, went back into a football game that he'd left after being badly shaken up near the end of the first half. A star player, he was returned to the game in the third quarter. On several plays he was noted to be lining up incorrectly. Near the end of the game, Zack was in on a big tackle at the goal line. It saved a victory for his teammates and school. When the game ended, Zack turned to his father, Victor, and said, "Dad, my head hurts." The next thing he said was, "I can't see."

Zack had suffered second impact syndrome. A concussion earlier in the game had not been recognized. A second blow to the head very nearly killed him. He lay in a coma for thirty days. Those chilling words — "I can't see" — were the last that Zack's parents heard him speak for nine months. But unlike most young athletes in his position, Zack survived.

Zack's recovery has been inspiring. In 2009, he returned to school. Two years later, he stood from his wheelchair, grabbed a cane, and walked across a stage to collect his high school diploma. He still has some distance to go in his recovery. His speech is slow and a bit slurred. Short-term memory is a challenge every day. The right side of his body isn't doing everything that he asks it to. Yet Zack is stirring change in remarkable ways. In 2009, the Washington State legislature passed the Zackery Lystedt Law. Similar legislation has now passed in more than thirty-three states. The National Football League, which has pushed for student-athlete concussion laws in all states, refers to the Lystedt Law as model legislation. The NFL highlights three provisions in the Lystedt Law that it is urging every state to adopt: coaches, parents and guardians, and athletes must receive concussion education and sign a concussion-information form; students suspected of having a concussion are required to immediately be removed from a game; before returning to play all concussed athletes must receive medical clearance from someone with training to recognize signs of head trauma. In states following the Lystedt model, these rules cover all athletes playing for middle and high school teams. In a few states, the laws reach deeper into youth sports. In Colorado, a concussion law pertains to private youth sports organizations such as Pop Warner Football and Little League Baseball.

The Lystedt Law was groundbreaking. It changed the concussions-in-youth-sports paradigm. Prior to passage of the law, a standard existed for handling head trauma — the "When in Doubt, Sit Them Out," approach discussed in an earlier chapter. It wasn't applied evenly, though. Some school districts observed the protocol to the letter. Others applied it sporadically. That left many kids unprotected.

The Lystedts were joined by a passionate group of advocates working for the cause. Stan Herring, clinical professor in the Department of Rehabilitation Medicine at the University of Washington, was the medical expert on the team while also serving as the team physician for the NFL Seattle Seahawks. He remembers meeting Zack and his parents for the first time — on the sidelines at Seahawks practice. The lawyer Richard Adler attended that practice with Zack. Adler is the former president of the Brain Injury Association of Washington. He built a broad coalition of support for the Lystedt Law among school sports groups, athletic trainers, and the state's largest youth soccer association. The Seahawks got behind the movement as well. But the most effective campaigner by far was Zack. As he has said to kids and parents, "If I could tell youth athletes one thing, it would be to take care of your health. If you're suspected of having a concussion, don't go back into the game, no matter how you feel when the adrenaline is flowing."

In 2009, the Washington house and senate passed the Lystedt Law without a dissenting vote. These laws will help educate millions of coaches, athletes, and parents. And they will protect millions of kids across the country. Traumatic brain injuries like the ones suffered by Zack Lystedt and Will Benson will not be eliminated. Only a law changing human nature could accomplish that. Some high school athletes will continue to play when their heads are hurting. As the years go by, fewer will put a football game ahead of their future. *That* will be progress.

In my home state of Massachusetts, a concussion law passed in 2010 follows the Lystedt model and goes farther. As in Washington State, a concussed athlete doesn't return to her sports team until she has been cleared by a physician or a certified athletic trainer or nurse practitioner in consultation with a physician. The Massachusetts law also requires a "graduated reentry plan" similar to the step-by-step approach used in our office. Few states require such a plan now, but that will change with time. The model is simple and patient-focused. The key players in a child's recovery work together to set a schedule, including a student's teacher, guidance counselor, school nurse, certified athletic trainer, parents, and physician. The child does not have a vote. Neither does her coach.

6

Chronic Traumatic Encephalopathy (CTE)

> I remember joking with him, "Wouldn't your brain make a nice specimen?" He started questioning whether he would have it himself. He told me that he wanted to donate his brain to the research when he died. Who would have thought that six months later it would be happening?
>
> — DANI PROBERT, wife of the former NHL player Bob Probert, who suffered from CTE (*New York Times*)

> Guys don't think about life down the road. They want the car. They want the bling. They want to have a nice life.
>
> — HARRY CARSON, Hall of Fame ex-linebacker who has post-concussion symptoms (*Time*)

MIKE WEBSTER WAS AN offensive lineman for the Pittsburgh Steelers in the 1970s — not just a lineman but a player so gifted that he later was elected to the Pro Football Hall of Fame. Webster's career spanned seventeen seasons at a position in which exposure to head trauma is nearly nonstop. His life after football was a sad window into the effects of such a relentless battering.

In 2002, Webster died at age fifty. Of twenty-two players who performed on all four Steelers Super Bowl teams of that era, he was the first to die. The cause of death was reported to be a heart attack. The real story was far more complicated and sobering. Three years before he died, Webster was found to have damage to the frontal lobe of his brain. His ability to think and to reason was profoundly affected. So were Webster's powers of attention and concentration.

In the final years of his life, Webster's injuries became incapacitating. His life was in ruins. Shortly before his Hall of Fame induction in 1997, a Pittsburgh newspaper reported that he was homeless, unemployed, deep in debt, and in the midst of a divorce. He acknowledged having spent nights in his car and a train station. His wife had taken a job as a cleaning woman.

A day after Webster's death, an autopsy was performed by the Allegheny County medical examiner's office. The pathologist who examined Webster's body was Dr. Bennet Omalu, an inquisitive and thorough man who noted on Webster's death certificate that his doctor had listed the cause of death as chronic brain injury. Dr. Omalu went to work to confirm (or dispel) this conclusion and determined that a contributing factor to Webster's death had been chronic traumatic encephalopathy, a disease of the brain previously seen in athletes only among prizefighters.

Dr. Omalu later shared his findings in a paper published in the journal *Neurosurgery,* the first time the disease had been cited in the death of a football player. The NFL's reaction was swift and dismissive. Three scientists affiliated with the league wrote to the journal editors demanding a retraction of Dr. Omalu's article. By then the Nigerian-born doctor had the brain of another recently deceased ex-Steeler. His name was Terry Long, and he had killed himself by drinking antifreeze. Dr. Omalu found that Long had CTE, the same progressive brain disease that he had found in Webster. He believed Long's erratic behavior and bouts of depression were linked to the diseased cells in his brain.

CTE is a progressive degenerative disease of the brain found in people exposed over many years to repetitive brain trauma. That trauma includes concussions, of course, and thousands upon thousands of subconcussive blows that athletes absorb over a lifetime playing left guard on a football team or right wing on an ice hockey squad. These jolts to the brain can trigger a buildup of an abnormal form of protein called tau. The process is similar to the one that takes place in the brains of Alzheimer's patients.

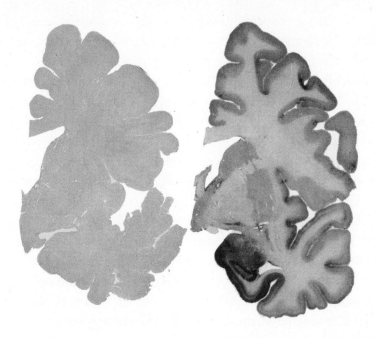

The normal brain *(left)* is free from deposits of abnormal tau, a toxic protein. The brain affected by CTE *(right)* shows a build-up of abnormal tau (very darkened areas). As the disease progresses, tau deposits clog pathways and damage axons.

The toxic abnormal tau proteins form plaques that block passageways in the brain, killing brain cells and destroying their axons.

The medial temporal lobe often comes under attack, causing victims to lose critical functions such as memory and impulse control. Patients who were strong, independent, and in command prior to the siege of CTE easily become depressed. Panic attacks are common, and as CTE advances, behavior can turn violent. The patients' brains turn to Swiss cheese and their lives unravel.

CTE is relatively new to the public discourse, but hardly a new disease. In 1928, Harrison Stanford Martland, the medical examiner of Essex County, New Jersey, wrote an article in the *Journal of the American Medical Association* that described a condition affecting prizefighters. The patients that Martland observed had symptoms that progressed over many years until eventually they became disabling. Victims suffered tremors, slowed movement, confusion, speech problems, a general decline in their thinking and reasoning. Martland named the condition dementia pugilistica. As time passed, others called it "punch-drunk syndrome." Now, it's CTE.

For decades after Martland's writing, it was surmised that among athletes only boxers risked dementia pugilistica because only boxers engaged in a line of work that involved years of climbing into a ring to be jabbed and punched. From the 1920s until the turn of the twenty-first century, not a single football or hockey player received the diagnosis.

The startling deaths of Mike Webster and Terry Long changed that. For a few days in a few places, the stories made headlines and began to move public opinion. The average fan was learning of the link between the violence they cheered on Sunday afternoons and the brain diseases their football heroes carried the rest of their lives. Chris Nowinski understood that well. At numerous stages of his life, he'd signed up for repetitive head trauma. At Harvard University, he'd played four years on the defensive line for the football team, using his size (six foot five) and smarts to become All–Ivy League at his position. After graduation, he'd chosen a bizarre career path for any college grad, and especially one with a Harvard degree. He entered the world of professional wrestling as a blond Adonis with chiseled pecs who went by the name "Chris Harvard."

Chris and I met in 2003 when he came to see me as a patient. Chris was in deep trouble. After a few years of being slammed by his opponents and anything else that could be dragged into the ring—including furniture—he was suffering a myriad of symptoms, including sleep disturbance, headaches, and memory loss. At our first meeting, we talked about how many concussions he had suffered during his wrestling and football days. He couldn't recall any and guessed that he might have had one. As we reviewed his history and he learned that being knocked out isn't necessary for a concussion to occur, that number grew to a half dozen or more. Chris learned quickly and developed a deep interest in what happened not only to him but to others with prolonged exposure to head trauma in sports. He and I hit it off and remained in touch, eventually working together to launch the Sports Legacy Institute, with Chris as CEO.

SLI is a nonprofit organization founded in 2007 to promote concussion awareness, prevention, treatment, and research, and in essence to solve the concussion crisis in sports. A year after the formation of SLI, we entered into a partnership with the Boston University School of Medicine to form the Center for the Study of Traumatic Encephalopathy (CSTE) and to pursue even more ambitious goals. In addition to Chris and myself, the co-directors are Dr. Ann McKee, then associate professor of neurology and pathology at BU and director of neuropathology for the New England Veterans Administration Healthcare System, and Dr. Robert Stern, an associate professor of neurology and the director of Clinical Core, Alzheimer's Disease Center, at BU. Due to the international recognition of the center, including more than ten scientific publications and many hundreds of presentations involving the directors, in three short years Dr. McKee and Dr. Stern have been elevated to full professors, and Chris, without missing a beat with his SLI work, is a graduate student working toward his PhD.

From left to right: Dr. Robert Stern, Dr. Ann McKee, Chris Nowinski, and Dr. Robert Cantu

The CSTE has three main areas of emphasis. One is a brain donation registry to which professional and amateur athletes from all sports commit to donating their brains after death so that they may be studied for disease, especially CTE. It is overseen by Dr. Stern, as is a longitudinal research grant from the National Institutes of Health in which athletes at high (such as NFL and NHL players) versus low risk of CTE are followed in the hope that we might find a reliable way to diagnose CTE in living patients. Among the tools that we are using for this purpose are biomarkers and advanced MRI imaging studies.

Finally, the third area of focus, and the one that has received most of the publicity to date, is the VA/BU CSTE Brain Bank, which, under Dr. McKee's leadership, is the world's largest athletic brain bank. In her lab, brains are studied.

In a way, these remarkable efforts owe their existence to a person who did not live to see them. His name was Andre Waters and he was an All-Pro defensive back for the Philadelphia Eagles and Arizona Cardinals from 1984 to 1995. In November 2006, Waters put a gun to his head and pulled the trigger. He died in his home in Tampa at the age of forty-four. After retiring from the NFL, Waters tried to catch on as a coach with a pro team, but nothing worked out, so he spent many years as an assistant coach with various small college squads.

As Alan Schwarz later reported in the *New York Times,* Chris saw a report of Waters's death that same day on the *Sports Illustrated* website, SI.com. He knew nothing about Waters the person. He knew a little about the player, mostly of his reputation as a hard hitter who gave out punishment and absorbed a lot too. Chris began researching Waters's career, with special interest in his head trauma. He discovered a 1994 newspaper article in which Andre was asked to count the concussions he had suffered. "I think I lost count at 15," he replied. "I just wouldn't say anything. I'd sniff some smelling salts, then go back in there."

Again, circumstances at the end of a football player's life pointed to

CTE. The only way to be certain was for an autopsy to be performed and for Andre's brain to be examined. Chris had never met any member of the Waters family. Yet he was so convinced that Andre's long history of head trauma had contributed to his death, even was the primary cause, that he picked up the phone and called Andre's mother, Willie Ola Perry. It's difficult to imagine the thoughts rushing through Chris's mind. He described it to the *Times* as "the most difficult cold-call [he'd] ever been a part of."

Chris received a return call from Andre's sister. He explained his belief that there was a connection between the deaths of Webster and Long and the violent end of her brother's life. After researching Chris's background and learning that he too had suffered multiple concussions as an athlete, the family gave its permission. Three weeks later, Dr. Omalu examined Waters's brain and confirmed that he had an advanced case of CTE.

Chris contacted Alan Schwarz, a reporter known for writing about complex issues surrounding sports as much as the games themselves. He laid out in detail for Alan what he had learned. In doing so, Chris helped set in motion the intense public debate that surrounds the issue today.

On January 18, 2007, the story of Waters's death appeared on the front page of the most influential newspaper in the world. Rather than fade away, as undoubtedly some NFL officials wished it would, the issue was gaining momentum and a sense of urgency.

In the early days of the Sports Legacy Institute, Chris and I had worked with Dr. Omalu. About this time, we decided to part ways. We formed a partnership with Dr. McKee to run the brain bank. She had a stellar reputation and, like us, lived and worked in the Boston area. In addition, we joined forces with Boston University to create the CSTE.

The new alliances gave us access to new resources and focused our work. In 2008 Dr. McKee confirmed CTE in the brains of two more deceased NFL players, Tom McHale and John Grimsley. Many more cases followed, each attracting more national attention.

By 2009, it was clear that head trauma in sports was far more than a sports story. Confirmation for me came in October when I was invited with Chris and Dr. McKee to testify at a hearing of the House Judiciary Committee in Washington, D.C. Others appearing before the committee included the NFL commissioner Roger Goodell, the NFL Players Association executive director DeMaurice Smith, Gay Culverhouse, former president of the Tampa Bay Buccaneers, and Merril Hoge, a former NFL player. Hoge told the committee that after his first concussion he never saw a doctor with training in head trauma and that he had been cleared to play in five days. It was an eye-opener for the committee. That was years ago — Hoge retired in 1994. He said, "What happened to me would not happen in the National Football League today." Still, former NFL players are more than concerned. In 2011, more than 120 players, including such stars as Jim McMahon, the free-spirited quarterback of the Chicago Bears in the 1990s, and Jamal Lewis, the star running back of the 2000 Super Bowl champion Baltimore Ravens, sued the league. The ex-players allege that the NFL and in some instances the manufacturers of helmets withheld information about the detrimental effects of repetitive head trauma. Several of the suits go further, saying that if the NFL didn't know, it had a duty to know and to protect the players.

CTE is not a disease that afflicts only aging professional athletes. Its victims can be younger, and sometimes much younger. In 2007, Nathan Stiles was a senior at Spring Hill High School in Kansas and an undisputed star. He played both offense and defense, as a running back and a linebacker, for the Broncos. It was a rare play in a Spring Hill game when number 44 was not on the field.

Nathan was more than a standout athlete. By all accounts he was a standout person. One classmate said of Nathan, "He was the most driven kid I ever knew. Everyone looked up to him." In his senior year, classmates voted Nathan homecoming king. After his death, ESPN produced a program about his life and his untimely death. Included in the show is a video of a "coronation" in which a pleased, if slightly sheepish, Nathan accepts his crown and strolls arm and arm with his mother before the Broncos' homecoming game. It seemed like a charmed life.

Until something went horribly wrong. On a Thursday evening, near the end of the first half of a Spring Hill game, Nathan intercepted a pass. He loped down the field until finally being dragged down, got to his feet, and walked to the sidelines. Then he collapsed. Nathan's coach told the local newspaper, "It was just a routine play. I don't think there was anything special. I think he just hit the ground pretty hard with his head. He came on the sideline and told one of my assistants, 'My head is really hurting.' He sat down on the bench. He then stood up, but his legs went out underneath him and collapsed there."

It wasn't Nathan's first blow to the head that season. Four weeks earlier, he suffered a concussion, sat out three games, and finally had returned to the Broncos lineup. On the sidelines, Nathan's condition slipped. He became unconscious, and doctors attending him called for a helicopter to airlift Nathan to a hospital in Kansas City. Nathan died there at four a.m. He was just seventeen years old.

After Nathan's death, his parents asked me to review his case. They wanted my opinion as to why Nathan had died. After reviewing health records and radiological studies, I was able to confirm the original explanation. Nathan had suffered a rebleed of a subdural hematoma and returned to the team while still injured. His brain hadn't been given time to heal.

After completing my work, I approached Mr. and Mrs. Stiles with a request for his brain to be examined at the Center for the Study of Traumatic Encephalopathy by Dr. McKee. Nathan's tragic death presented an opportunity that we rarely have at the center — to search for CTE in the brain of a teenage athlete showing no outward signs of the disease. In effect, I was asking Mr. and Mrs. Stiles for their help with a crucial research question. Is the repetitive trauma that our kids are taking in collision sports such as tackle football and ice hockey starting the process that results in degenerative brain disease? Can teen athletes have CTE?

The Stiles family had just been through an unfathomable nightmare, one that would not be over soon, if ever. Yet they were quick to respond, giving permission for Nathan's brain to be studied. They also sent medical records including CT scans of his brain.

"It's not going to matter for Nathan, but it might for someone else," Connie Stiles, Nathan's mom, told ESPN at the time.

Dr. McKee's examination revealed what we suspected — and feared. Although it was at an early stage, Nathan's brain had CTE. The disease certainly hadn't been the cause of his death. (A CT scan of his brain showed that Nathan possibly died of second impact syndrome in addition to the subdural rebleed.)

As of this writing, Nathan is the youngest person ever diagnosed with CTE, but not the only young athlete. Dr. McKee also has confirmed the disease in the brains of Eric Pelly, eighteen, and Owen Thomas, twenty-one. Eric suffered a concussion in a rugby match when he was bashed in the temple with another player's knee. He was hospitalized for three days and released. A week later he was having dinner with his family, collapsed at the table, and died. Eric was a kid who craved contact. In addition to rugby, as rough a sport as football considering it's played with virtually no protective equipment, he played football, hockey, baseball, and basketball. In 2010, Owen, a star defensive end on the University of Pennsylvania's varsity football team, committed suicide several weeks after being named a team captain. Outwardly, Owen had seemed fine to coaches and teammates, none of whom recalled behavior that was out of the ordinary. Whether CTE contributed to his decision to end his life is unclear. (Given the early stage of the disease, it is doubtful.) Yet there's no argument that Owen had been a football player most of his life and had taken many knocks to the head — but never sustained a recognized concussion!

At the Center for the Study of Traumatic Encephalopathy, the work goes on. So far, more than three hundred brains have been pledged for study; many are players whose professional careers were spent in the most violent sports — football and ice hockey. We have no brains for our research from athletes in basketball, baseball, tennis, golf, field hockey, and lacrosse. Just one brain from a female athlete has been examined as I write this. These are critical gaps in our research.

Thus far, Dr. McKee and her team have detected fifty-eight cases of CTE. Thirty-one of those cases involve football players, and a rising number are hockey players. We received the brains of four former National Hockey League players, Bob Probert, Reg Fleming, Derek Boogaard, and Rick Martin. Probert, Fleming, and Boogaard were enforcer types. Over their careers they were at the center of thousands of scuffles and hundreds of actual fights on the ice. They took slams in the head countless times. Probert's style of play was so rough that he and a brawling teammate were known as the "Bruise Brothers." Martin was involved in one of the worst accidents in hockey history while playing for the Buffalo Sabres. After banging his head on the ice, he was knocked unconscious and went into convulsions. When he died in 2009, Fleming was seventy-three. Martin died at age sixty. Probert at forty-five. Boogaard at just twenty-eight. All four had CTE.

CTE is life-altering for its victims and the families faced with the enormous responsibility of caring for them. A painful role reversal occurs and the dad counted on as breadwinner and a family's center of gravity now is the one whose needs others must struggle to meet twenty-four/seven. As the cases of Webster and Long sadly show, these patients can be a threat not only to themselves but to the people who love them most.

One can only imagine life with the professional wrestler Chris Benoit in his last years. From 2000 to 2007, Benoit appeared on the biggest cards and packed the biggest arenas for his bouts in the World Wrestling Federation and later World Wrestling Entertainment, the big leagues of the sport. Benoit wasn't huge for his profession — five foot eleven, and 220 pounds — but he was a showman and he was tough, the kind of guy who'd land on his head, shake off the cobwebs and pin his opponent, then have a chair slammed across his head as he left the ring. The tougher Benoit's act, the more his fans loved it.

But on June 22, 2007, something in Benoit's brain snapped. In his home in Atlanta, he strangled his wife, Nancy, leaving a Bible beside her body. Then he murdered his son, Daniel, who was seven years old. He placed a Bible beside Daniel's body as well. Chris Benoit then ended his own life by hanging himself. The reasons for Benoit's deranged acts are not known. Steroids reportedly were found in his home, stoking speculation that the murders happened while Benoit was in a "steroid rage." If so, then Benoit's sanity was under assault from several directions that day. Not only was CTE detected in his brain, but on Dr. McKee's one-to-four rating system, Chris Benoit's CTE was a four.

Pro athletes worry about CTE. In their daily lives things happen to them — they misplace their car keys or momentarily forget the name of a friend — and they wonder what it means. Is it an early sign of a degenerative brain disease? Are they walking around with CTE?

Often former athletes will come into the office and tell me their stories. They're doing well in their business and have great families. Life is good and they seem to be functioning at a high level. An incident or two of forgetfulness has unsettled them. They think they are okay, but they come in for confirmation and reassurance.

Memory loss is a part of aging. You can have a very healthy brain and forget an appointment now and then. If that's what's bugging them, they can relax. I can't tell these folks that they don't have CTE. There isn't a test I can give that will conclusively rule out this possibility. And neither is it prudent to assure a patient by telling him he will never get CTE. How could we know that? If I am concerned, I will give the person a neurological exam. If the results are normal, that can be quite reassuring.

It's a different story if a person comes in with a complaint of "My wife says I'm forgetting all day, every day." That is not normal. We want to do a thorough workup of those patients to determine what is occurring and why. For those who are quite impaired, we do all that's possible to help.

Given the national debate about CTE, it is not surprising that younger patients fear it too. High school athletes who have had multiple concussions are concerned not just about their headache today. They want to know whether their brains already have been invaded by the disease.

Chris Vanesian was a two-sport athlete in high school and hoped to continue playing in college. Concussions had set him back repeatedly. In two and a half years, he suffered three concussions and quite possibly four.

During his recoveries, Chris tells me, he frequently wondered whether his concussion history increased his risk for CTE. When we spoke recently, Chris acknowledged that he still worries.

"Could I be affected when I'm fifty and hopefully have my own kids? Every day, it's in the back of my mind," he tells me.

That concern lingers after patients have recovered from their concussions and go back to their regular lives. There's a feeling of helplessness and an even greater sense of vulnerability. It's impossible to know whether lasting damage has been done. The reality is that even if this could be known, it would not be helpful. No treatment exists for arresting the progression of CTE. "There's nothing I can do at this point," explains T.J. Cooney, who had multiple concussions while playing varsity football for Catholic University and was forced to give up the sport. "I had no idea that it could become an issue. Now I try to lead a healthy lifestyle and take every precaution I can. But yeah, I'm scared."

The concern of those athletes and their parents is understandable. As stated throughout this book, no head trauma is good head trauma. Yet the avalanche of publicity about concussions in recent years has distorted the connection — the public's perception of the connection — between concussions and CTE. As we understand it, CTE is caused by total brain trauma, which includes concussions but is not limited to them. Athletes in most sports are exposed to a far greater number of subconcussive blows. These are the lighter slams and bangs that lack the force of a concussion but still jar the brain. Kids playing collision sports can register more than a thousand in a season. Over many years, they can accumulate tens of thousands. It happens before our eyes, and unless our child complains of a headache or a dizzy spell, we rarely notice.

The challenge that we face as parents, coaches, and physicians is exposing kids to the great life lessons that sports offer without exposing their heads to the tap, tap, and occasional pop that may lead to CTE.

The Sports Legacy Institute strongly backs efforts that work toward that goal. Specific proposals are needed, and several will be recommended and argued for later in this book.

Do high school football players need daily full-contact workouts to be ready to play on Friday night or Saturday? Are girls' lacrosse and field hockey players safer when they *aren't* wearing helmets? It's time to decide.

I asked Sylvia Mackey for her views about keeping sports safer. Like few people I know, Sylvia understands the complexities of the issue. Her late husband, John, was one of the truly great players in professional football during his career as a tight end for the Baltimore Colts in the 1960s and went into the Pro Football Hall of Fame as one of the best to ever play his position. Yet the last years of his life were a shocking contrast. Mackey suffered a degenerative brain disease. In 2011, he died at the age of sixty-nine.

Through Sylvia's efforts, the NFL began to respond to ex-players whose families were struggling to care for them. In 2007, Sylvia wrote a letter to then NFL commissioner Paul Tagliabue, explaining her plight. She simply could not keep up with the expenses related to John's illness. Tagliabue was moved by Sylvia's appeal and several months later the NFL launched Plan 88, named for the number that Mackey wore throughout his NFL career. Any ex-player that has a degenerative brain disease can apply for an annual payment to help cover the costs of his care. Recently, the NFL extended the benefit to individuals with amyotrophic lateral sclerosis, Lou Gehrig's disease. The amount: $88,000.

As it turned out, Sylvia's husband didn't have CTE. Dr. McKee made a diagnosis of frontal temporal dementia, an unrelated condition. Yet Sylvia has been an outstanding advocate for players and their families struggling to care for their loved ones.

Despite the loss of her husband and all that she has witnessed in other families, Sylvia isn't anti-football. She believes the sport has much to offer young people. "Football is a good sport. I don't think you can stop it. I don't support taking anything out of it," she said. "Parents and kids have to be educated about what they're getting into. Then let them make their own decision."

That's exactly what happened in Sylvia Mackey's family. Sylvia and John's daughter, Lisa, has two sons; at the time their grandfather became ill their ages were ten and twelve. Both were playing in organized football leagues where they live in Bowie, Maryland.

After John's diagnosis, the family made some changes: "My daughter took them both out of football. Her attitude was, they can play basketball," Sylvia explained. Ben Hazel, the older of Lisa's two boys, took that advice and ran with it all the way to Princeton University, where he is a member of the varsity basketball squad. No doubt John Mackey would be proud.

Despite the newfound attention, CTE research still is at an early stage. Among our goals at the Center for the Study of Traumatic Encephalopathy is to develop a test for CTE in living patients and to identify genetic predictors of the disease. There may be environmental triggers. We are studying that, too.

To a large extent, our progress depends on continued support of the brain bank. When the center wasn't widely known, donations were more difficult to come by, and we worked hard to spread the message of our work. Chris Nowinski did a fantastic job meeting with families and using his flair for public speaking to elevate the profile of the center. All of us connected with the research have done our part to ensure that donors know where to find us. That was brought home to all of us in a powerful way in 2011 when we learned of the death of Dave Duerson, a former NFL player who was just fifty years old. Before he fired a bullet into his chest, Duerson wrote a suicide note to his family that read: PLEASE, SEE THAT MY BRAIN IS GIVEN TO THE N.F.L.'S BRAIN BANK. The family honored the request and Dave's brain was sent to Dr. McKee's lab at the VA/BU CSTE Brain Bank in Bedford, Massachusetts. Her analysis revealed CTE.

7

Myths

I thought they were a football injury — a boy thing. Those guys are taught to hit hard and knock people to the ground. But anyone can get a concussion, and I don't think a lot of girls recognize that.

— HANNAH STOLLER, a soccer player at Conard High School in West Hartford, Connecticut (*New York Times*)

DESPITE GROWING AWARENESS of concussions and the dangers they pose, misconceptions remain. Some contain a grain of truth but have been amplified and distorted over the years. Others are absolutely and unequivocally wrong. It's important to set the record straight.

"You can't have a concussion without being hit in the head, can you?"

A dozen times each year, a perplexed mom or dad will ask that question. It's one of several myths about concussions that are impossible to stamp out.

The parents are concerned that their child has suffered a concussion. He has been complaining of a headache for several days. He's not himself: irritable, sluggish, lacking the usual energy and enthusiasm.

All signs seem to point to head trauma, yet it doesn't seem possible. A youth baseball pitcher doesn't get a sore elbow running the bases. How can a young linebacker get a concussion without a blow to his head?

In fact, many concussions occur without direct contact to the head. They're caused by rotational forces or accelerations — the head whips to one side and the brain shifts inside the skull, bruising when it bangs against the hard ridged surface or being stretched to the point of injury. We refer to this as the "whiplash effect" — a hard blow to the chest snaps the head violently forward and a hard blow from behind will snap the head back. The rotational forces that are generated can cause a concussion without a direct hit to the head.

In this chapter, I'm sharing a few of the myths that I hear often in my office — and the myth-busting facts that every coach and parent should know.

To have a concussion, you need to be knocked unconscious.

That would be news to the 95 percent of athletes who have had concussions and did not lose consciousness. There's not a shred of truth to it.

So why do many of us think of *concussion* as a synonym for *out cold*? Years ago, concussions had a more limited meaning and almost always came up in the context of an automobile or motorcycle crash. The victim bashed his head against the steering wheel. The impact was severe, and when police arrived they found the driver hunched forward, passed out cold. This image was perpetuated by a generation of crime dramas — every episode ended with a bad guy turned upside down in his getaway car, completely knocked out.

By contrast, concussions seldom came up in a conversation about sports, even one about sports injuries. A player who'd been hit in the head was "dinged" or "had his "bell rung." Lou Gehrig, the baseball legend of the 1920s and '30s, supposedly was once beaned with a pitch so hard that he lay on the ground motionless for five minutes. Despite a terrible headache, Gehrig played the next day wearing Babe Ruth's larger cap to cover a bump on his head. None of the newspaper accounts of the game mentioned even the possibility of a concussion.

It would seem that a concussion that knocks out the injured athlete is more serious than one that doesn't. But in fact that's inaccurate too, according to many studies that have looked at that question.

Helmets prevent most concussions.

Don't get me wrong: Helmets are important, even essential equipment in collision sports. In the rougher sports — football, hockey, men's lacrosse, baseball (for batting) — they provide excellent protection against a blow that is focal. That is, the force is concentrated in a small area.

Here's an example. Your son is a lacrosse attack man. He charges down the field and blows by a defenseman on his way to the goal. As he whooshes past, the defender swings his stick, smashing the carbon-fiber shaft across your child's helmet. If it does what it's supposed to do, the hard shell of the helmet spreads the force of the blow over a wider area. This dampens the force, reducing the possibility of concussion, dramatically reducing the chance for bleeding of the brain, and virtually eliminating skull fractures.

But helmets have real limitations and should not be regarded as the solution. Consider another situation. Your daughter, a star ice hockey defenseman, is racing full speed from one end of the rink to the other in pursuit of a loose puck. Just as she gets her stick on it, she loses her balance and slams into the boards. There's no contact with her head. The blow catches her on the shoulder. Her head whips from one side to another, twisting and torquing the structures of the brain. She may be wearing a new helmet. It may be the most advanced in terms of fit and padding. It may be the most expensive on the market. Yet helmets offer little or no protection against accelerations resulting from this type of hit.

In addition, the more the hit is "off center," the less the helmet can protect the player. Imagine an offensive lineman in football taking a hit on the side of the helmet or, worse, the tip of the facemask. The facemask acts as a lever, increasing rotational forces and stresses on the brain.

A few years ago, the National Football League adopted new rules for tackling the quarterback. Restrictions were put in place making it illegal for charging linemen and blitzing linebackers to strike the quarterback in the helmet. Recently this has been expanded to include not just the quarterback but anyone in the act of throwing the football.

Quarterbacks needed more protection — that was clear. They were being sidelined with concussions at an alarming rate. It was a bad situation for the NFL because the league has a stake in protecting players, especially star players who draw in fans.

The rule reduced concussions caused by direct blows to the head. No longer were pass rushers crashing into quarterbacks, swatting at their helmets with their huge hands. And no longer were quarterbacks being hit from their "blind side," also a positive. Such hits leave players no chance to tense their neck and otherwise brace themselves in the nanosecond before the collision.

The new rule hasn't prevented quarterbacks from getting concussions, though. They're still being wrestled to the ground. And they're still slamming into the turf as violently as ever — in ways that trigger rotational forces. The league's efforts were helpful to a point. But thus far, they haven't defeated the laws of physics.

The next concussion is always more serious than the last.

This statement would be true if it were stated like so: The next concussion is more serious than the last — *except when it isn't.* Every concussion is unique. It's not possible to generalize and be right more than half the time.

The best way to explain is by sharing two stories.

Willie Baun was a young football player who came to my office about ten years ago. At the time, Willie was twelve years old and had been playing in an organized tackle football league since the age of seven. The coach of every one of those teams was his father, Whitey.

Willie had had a rough year. Early in the season, he leaped after a football, trying to recover an onside kick, and suffered a concussion. Another player coming from a different direction was doing the same thing at the same time. Unfortunately for both, their helmets cracked. Willie walked off the field and appeared to be fine. But watching his son on the field, Whitey sensed something was wrong, so he insisted that his son go to the bench for the rest of the game.

Something *was* wrong. After the game, Whitey and his wife, Becky, took their son to the hospital and learned that he had a concussion. He needed to take off three weeks and maybe longer, depending on whether his headaches had eased. After three weeks, Willie's symptoms had not disappeared, a clear signal that it is too soon for any athlete — particularly a child of ten — to return to play. Yet Willie's parents weren't aware that allowing their son to rejoin his team was a risky decision. Five weeks after the initial concussion, Willie was practicing with the team, doing a drill that wasn't that strenuous, when he was tapped on the head by a teammate, a glancing blow at best. Almost certainly, Willie's earlier concussion (from which he likely had returned to play too soon) had turned the relatively light blow into something serious. This time, Willie's symptoms were many times worse, among the worst I have seen. His deficits were incredible. Suddenly Willie couldn't remember the names of his classmates, couldn't retrieve the right words, couldn't do the simplest math problems. In Willie's case, the second concussion clearly was worse than the first.

Now the story of Patrice Bergeron, star hockey player for the Boston Bruins. Patrice suffered three concussions over a relatively short period of time — three years. Each concussion was recorded on video. So unlike most kids whose concussions I am treating, we have pictures of what happened to Patrice.

In the first, he's standing about two feet from the glass and gets rammed from behind. His head is driven into the glass and virtually shatters it. He is knocked unconscious and has to be carried off the ice.

On the second, he's blindsided, hit by an elbow on the side of the jaw. He drops in a heap but within a few seconds scrambles to his feet. Within a minute or two, he's able to skate (in wobbly fashion) off the ice.

Patrice's third concussion was caused by another blow to the side of the head, a light blow compared with the others.

Consider Bergeron's recovery from these concussions. After the first concussion, he was lost to the Bruins for the season — his symptoms persisted for four and a half months. After the second concussion, the symptoms lasted fourteen days and he was out of the lineup for a month. The symptoms from the third disappeared in four days. He was back on the ice in two weeks.

Multiple concussions are reason for concern. They can lower the brain's resistance to the next concussion and the next. If a patient has severe symptoms caused by a relatively mild blow, it suggests that her brain is approaching a threshold. I sit down with the athlete and her parents and have a serious talk, one that no one is looking forward to. If she plays multiple collision sports, the advice may be to pick one. Depending on her concussion history, the best course might be to give up all collision sports.

But that's not all patients. It's just not possible to generalize.

Three concussions and your child's career in collision sports is over.

There isn't a magic number that should end a child's career. The analysis is more complicated.

Your child's doctor should consider several factors in addition to how many concussions a young athlete has suffered. They include the gap in time between concussions, the severity of the concussions, and the relationship between the head trauma and the symptoms that followed. In other words, did a blow that was quite minor cause lots of very intense symptoms? That indicates a lowering of resistance to head trauma and needs to be taken seriously.

Of the factors mentioned, the most important is the severity of the head trauma. Willie Baun, the young man mentioned earlier, had nine months of profound memory loss after his one and only concussion — aggravated by a second hit while he still had symptoms. His situation was so serious that we agreed that he would stop playing collision sports. (Willie was able to return to non-collision sports, however.) Other athletes are able to bounce back quickly again and again. This may be due to the amount of time that has passed between their injuries — long intervals between head trauma assist in recovery. Or maybe it is simply due to our physiology, the differences among us.

Before an athlete is cleared to play again, he must be symptom-free while resting and exercising. If symptoms return during a light workout in the gym, it's time to back off and to reset the recovery clock. The athlete hasn't recovered until he is symptom-free at rest and at exertion — back to whatever "normal" was before the concussion.

Concussions determine risk of chronic traumatic encephalopathy (CTE).

Total brain trauma is the best predictor of developing CTE. Concussions certainly result in brain trauma, so they count. Yet so does subconcussive trauma, blows to the head that are potentially damaging yet not strong enough to cause concussions.

To a great extent, the public views the concussion — the poster child of head trauma — as the gateway to feared brain diseases including CTE. Concussions generate buzz and get all the publicity. For my patients who've had multiple concussions and fear that they are at risk for developing CTE later in life, I offer simple advice: Relax. The connection has been greatly overstated.

Boys suffer more concussions than girls.

Boys will be boys, right? They play rougher than girls. So they suffer more concussions. Several recent studies suggest this is false.

In 2007, an ambitious research project led by Dawn Comstock of Ohio State reported this data:

In high school soccer, the girls' concussion rate was 68
    percent higher than the rate for boys.
In high school basketball, the concussion rate for girls
    was three times higher than for boys.

The 2007 study also found that recovery time for girls was longer than for boys.

In 2011, Comstock published a second research study with results that confirmed what the first had shown. In high school soccer, the concussion rate for girls (0.35 per 1,000 participations by an athlete in a practice or game) was double the rate for boys (.017). In basketball the concussion rate for girls was nearly two times higher than for boys.

How is the disparity explained? Comstock and the study's other authors question whether athletic trainers pay more attention to female athletes than males because "society has tended to be more protective of female athletes."

The results also suggest the following:

- **Differences in training.** In ice hockey, boys are permitted to body check at a certain age while girls are not. It may be that boys' bodies are trained to handle those blows because they're a part of the game earlier and they have to learn to deal with them. Girls aren't accustomed to being smashed against the boards. They're not as prepared to handle that degree of contact.
- **Differences in body type.** Most boys have bigger, stronger necks than girls. A less developed neck definitely is a risk factor.
- **Cultural differences.** Boys are brought up to shrug off injuries. Be tough. Be stoic.

It is different for girls. It is accepted that girls report how they are feeling to coaches, athletic trainers, and parents. There's no stigma, no cultural penalty.

If these differences are real, as I believe they are, they raise intriguing questions about concussion studies. Are those focused on gender reliable? How different would the picture be if all concussions were counted, not just those that youth athletes report to coaches and athletic trainers? For now, let's hang an asterisk on this myth.

Mouth guards prevent concussions.

"The single most important value of a mouth guard is the concussion saving effect following impact to the mandible (lower jaw). Ninety-five per cent of all football concussions are transmitted through the mandible to the brain. Therefore, the use of athletic mouth guards should be encouraged in all contact sports. Mouth guards serve as a shock absorber to help prevent concussions and possibly brain injuries."

That statement is pasted directly from the website of a company that sells athletic mouth guards. This particular mouth guard sells for $49.95. It seems like a reasonable price for a device that makes a big promise like "possibly" preventing brain injury. There's little doubt that many parents have purchased them for their children for that reason.

If that was the motivation, they threw away fifty bucks. There is absolutely no scientific basis for the claim. Accelerations cause concussions and they are transmitted directly to the brain — the mouth guard is not involved. Many football concussions are caused by rotational forces — a player takes a shot to the helmet and his head spins. It doesn't spin or move less because he's wearing a mouth guard.

What I've said sounds like a repudiation of mouth guards and isn't meant to. Mouth guards have real value — protecting mouths. In some high school sports, simple mouth guards (not the $49.95 models) are required to be on the field. They have nothing to do with preventing concussions, however, no matter what you may have read.

Concussion symptoms are obvious as soon as a
concussion occurs.

This is true of many symptoms. It's not true of all.

Again, let's consider some examples. An ice hockey goalie is slammed in the goal crease, falls, and bounces her head on the ice. If the goalie has a concussion, it's likely that a number of symptoms will come on rather quickly, including a headache, nausea, perhaps a feeling of being stunned or disoriented.

This statement earns a place among other classic myths because concussion symptoms aren't always obvious right away. Take the case of a high school soccer player who suffers a concussion in a heading mishap. The accident occurs over Thanksgiving break. When the player goes back to school in a few days, it takes longer to complete his homework assignments. He's having considerable trouble concentrating. The concussed player probably has had the symptom for some time. A cognitive test given at the time of the concussion might have revealed it. Yet because he wasn't in a situation in which mental focus was needed, he was unaware.

The message for parents and coaches is to be alert for symptoms when concussions occur. Then continue to be alert for another week. If your child has a concussion, symptoms should be evident by then.

8

Moms and Dads

If I'm a parent, I should be worried that my school has no athletic trainer. To me, that's insane.

— ROBERT SALLIS, a Southern California physician and
past president of the American College of Sports Medicine
(*San Jose Mercury News*)

KATHY GALLAGHER HAS more experience than she'd like observing concussions and concussion symptoms. Her knowledge comes from watching her daughter, Mary Kate.

When Mary Kate was twelve, she was playing in a school basketball game. She'd heard that the girl she would be defending played "super aggressive," and the scouting report was entirely accurate. With about twenty minutes left in the game, the girl made a move down the lane and slammed into Mary Kate. The girl's forehead smashed Mary Kate in the right temple. That was concussion one. In the tangle of bodies, Mary Kate lost her balance and went tumbling to the floor, hitting the back of her head on the court. Within a few seconds, she'd suffered a second concussion.

Mary Kate's symptoms were all in the realm of physical setbacks — headaches, lightheadedness, and balance deficits. Her recovery went smoothly and in three weeks she was feeling nearly back to normal.

Seven months later, Mary Kate was playing lacrosse for a private school team where she lives near Boston. During a game, a teammate took a hard shot on goal and instead slammed the ball into Mary Kate's head from a very short distance — two to three feet. The

Mary Kate Gallagher

point of impact was her left temple, the opposite side from where she'd been slammed in the basketball game. Just as with the previous concussions, Mary Kate had a significant number of symptoms, only this time her emotional state was also affected. She was uncharacteristically nervous and irritable. Often, little things became big things. When her mom asked her to pitch in with routine household chores, she could be short and uncooperative. "She was just not herself," says Kathy. "As her parent, I recognized the changes. I'm not sure others would."

Call it a sixth sense or a parent knowing her child through and through. Whatever the explanation, moms and dads have an ability to note small behavioral changes long before they would be picked up by others, including a family physician. That state of hyperawareness may not seem like an asset in life around the house. In reading a child for the possibility of concussion, it absolutely is.

Some changes in a child's demeanor naturally point to a concussion or suspicion of one. A child coming home from hockey practice with complaints of double vision hasn't left much to interpretation. The young person should be checked out as soon as possible. Most changes are harder to read, and they include a child who is solemn or subdued, whose appetite is different (eating more or less than unusual), and whose sleep patterns suddenly change. All are warning signs.

Kathy Gallagher's daughter normally was a patient young woman. After her second concussion, though, Kathy recalls, the family was "walking on eggshells" around her. "Things that wouldn't provoke a reaction before suddenly bothered her a lot," Kathy tells me. "It might be as simple as 'It's time to get ready for bed.' You never knew." Mary Kate remembers battling with her younger brother (with whom she usually gets along well) over issues as small as passing a dinner plate. Afterward, she'd wonder why. "The slightest thing ticked me off," she tells me.

Parents shouldn't attempt to diagnose concussions. That's a job for physicians trained to manage head trauma. That does not exclude moms and dads from the important job of studying children for signs. When a child has a concussion the clock begins to tick. The sooner she gets to the doctor and receives proper treatment, the better the outcome. If she is seen by a physician in the first few days, chances are there will be fewer symptoms to deal with and they will be milder. If she doesn't and returns to the stress of school, she could be set up for a prolonged recovery. Going back to sports is even worse.

Use every tool in the parental toolbox. This includes a series of simple tests that can be given at home as easily as in my office. The training needed is minimal and there are no insurance forms to fill out.

Imagine your son is a football player. Playing in a game, he took several shots to the head. There's nothing obvious in his behavior to indicate that he suffered a concussion, but you're concerned and unsure. A common concussion symptom is a deficit in short-term memory. That can be tested easily by a parent by posing a series of questions about recent events. If you'd rather stick with the neurosurgeon's template, here are several suggestions. Whatever questions are chosen, be sure that the test giver is confident of the answers. (Sometimes this step is overlooked.)

The questions can be this simple:

What was the score of the last game?
What team were you playing?
What were the colors of the jerseys worn by the opposing team?

There are other ways to test orientation. A dad might ask a kid to choose four unrelated words — such as object names or colors. Ask the child to repeat the list. Then say, "I'm going to ask you to repeat that again in three or four minutes. Let's see if you can do that for me." It becomes a game with real value in identifying a problem.

A mom can tick off six digits for the child. Then she can ask the child to repeat those six digits back, giving them at roughly one-second intervals. If the child can repeat six digits forward — as in, 6-9-9-9-7-0, move to the next level and ask her to repeat the numbers backwards.

Asking a child how he's feeling is a question, not a test. And it's a question that occurs so naturally to a parent that it hardly needs to be recommended. What may be less clear are appropriate follow-ups that reveal more about a child's condition. Continue the conversation with prompts such as *Are you having trouble with memory? Have you noticed issues with concentration? Is your homework taking longer? Is doing homework causing a headache that it wouldn't normally? When you study for longer periods, does the headache get worse?*

At the extremes, it's usually evident what the next steps should be. If a child sails through each evaluation without a sign of a deficit, probably there isn't a need to go further. Observe your child closely for another day or two to confirm the earlier impression. At the other end of the spectrum, the same is true. If a question about yesterday's game stumps your child and she struggles to keep her balance with eyes closed, there's reason for concern. Find a physician who has training in concussions. Take the first appointment available.

The cases in between are more difficult. There's no foolproof formula for deciding when it is time to bring in your child to be evaluated. My view is that a child should be seen if he is trying as hard as he can yet struggles to complete cognitive or balance tests. It may be that everything is fine and that the visit was not needed. It may be. Yet in our office, it is relatively rare that a parent brings in a child to be seen for the wrong reasons.

The inconvenience and cost involved in having a child checked out is relatively low. The price to that child if he has had a concussion and it is overlooked would be very high. That one visit may save a child from losing a year or more in school. That one affirmative act may save a child's life. A few children each year die from second impact syndrome.

How should a parent choose a doctor? It's a question that many parents face, and it's important in determining quality of care. Certainly, most pediatricians and family-practice doctors are excellent at treating the issues they see in their offices each day. On concussions, they may have the necessary background and training — and they may not.

Concussion training is new in the medical field. The majority of doctors in practice now received little or no education about it in medical school, internship, and residency training. What they know has been picked up recently in medical journals, online courses, and in lectures at continuing education meetings. Surprisingly — and sadly — even neurologists (who treat disorders of the brain) have had scant education in athletic concussions.

The old way of thinking was that concussions were serious but that eventually everyone recovered. As long as the doctor ruled out a subdural hematoma — a bleed in the brain — everything would be fine. We've since learned that's not the whole story. Patients need cognitive and physical rest after a concussion, and when they don't get it, symptoms last a lot longer.

Without proper care, the average person is set up for a few more weeks of misery dealing with symptoms and the inconvenience of missing valuable time at work or in school. For an athlete, the stakes are higher. An athlete whose concussion is untreated or treated improperly is exposing herself to serious injury. And she probably has no idea. That athlete may go back on a field and have another head injury that's permanently disabling or even fatal. Concussion deaths from second impact syndrome are rare, but they happen each year.

How should you choose a physician? Personal relationships and the recommendations of friends are valuable, but they're not as important as the doctor's training in athletic concussions. Some medical practices cite this sort of information on websites or other places that are accessible to the general public. If they don't, there's only one other way to find out about their backgrounds, and that's to ask.

Some patients and parents of patients will be uncomfortable speaking about credentials with their doctor, and I understand. It feels to them as if they're auditioning the doctor, even challenging his ability to make a proper diagnosis. The reality is that few physicians will take it that way. Most will respect that you're an advocate for your son or daughter and focused only on getting the best care. When you do run into the doctor who gets his hackles up, simply thank him for his time and move on. That doctor shouldn't be treating head trauma patients anyway.

In our office at Emerson Hospital, a parent almost always accompanies a child to an appointment. That is the case even with high school–aged children. And these days, with concussion awareness growing, often we see both parents. Frequently, I'll turn to Mom and Dad and ask, "What you have noticed?" They may not think that they can add much to the picture, but often they do. Changes may seem too insignificant to mention, but the smallest detail helps, and moms and dads have lots of them.

The patients are led through a series of exams that verify deficits that we know they have and others we may not. These include a "mini-mental" exam such as the memory games mentioned earlier, an assessment of any visual impairment, and of course a balance check. The most common physical neurologic abnormality right after a concussion is loss of balance.

Before and after the exam, patients and their families often are asking a long list of questions, all getting at the same point: *When is this going to be over? When will I feel better?* Often, they've been sick for several months and their symptoms have had a grinding-down effect. They are seeking any sort of hope and looking to their doctor for answers. There isn't a mortal who can give these patients the answers they're seeking. The best we can do is to offer predictions based on the pace of their recovery thus far. So, looking at the previous six weeks often can be a clue for predicting what may lie ahead in the next six weeks. If the progress has been slow, it may continue to be slow.

Whatever the results, I tell the patient that he is almost certainly going to get better. In my office, we've been seeing concussion patients for decades. We had a person with post-concussion syndrome that lasted five years. Slowly, slowly, that patient recovered. It's difficult for some patients to imagine being normal again; they have been so challenged by their symptoms. My message is "You will get better."

The patients we see are a diverse group, far more so than in years past. In 1972, high school sports were dominated by boys; they outnumbered girls by twelve to one. Then came the passage of Title IX and a change not only in the law but our collective attitude about equality for girls on playing fields. By 2011, that disparity had shrunk to 1.3 boys for each girl. Our patients reflect that change. For better or worse, gender parity has been achieved in our office.

The age of our patients also has changed. As in the past, the majority are high school athletes who've been banged up playing collision sports, usually football, ice hockey, and lacrosse. Now we're seeing much younger children. The youngest children I have treated for sports-related head trauma are five, six, and seven years old. Some are victims of mishaps at home or on the playground. An increasing number, though, are injured playing organized sports. I've seen many football players in this age group and hockey players nearly as young. I haven't seen five-year-old soccer players for concussion. At that age kids are running around a huge field and occasionally kicking a ball. The most dangerous play — heading the ball — begins later.

Parents are the best line of defense that a child can have for the reasons stated throughout this book. The large and small sacrifices they make to speed the recoveries of their children are impressive. (One mom told me recently she'd searched for her daughter's five favorite books on CD because reading aggravated her headaches.) It would be misleading, though, to say that all moms and dads have gotten the message. Frankly, some have not. Often, they're well-intentioned people who become wrapped up in the excitement of raising a star player.

Once, a young hockey player at a prestigious high school came in to see me after being diagnosed with a concussion. It was his fourth, and I had treated him for those earlier concussions as well. In fact, I'd seen him about two months earlier for a concussion from which he had recovered and been cleared to return to sports.

The young man's parents accompanied their son to the office for this appointment, and they were present when I questioned him about what happened.

"About three weeks ago, I'm on the ice when a big guy suddenly skates over, hits me, and rubs me against the glass," he told me.

As I listened, I remember thinking, *That's an interesting choice of words.* To me, "rub" isn't the same as "slam" or "wallop" or "shove headfirst into the glass." It's a little less violent than that. Maybe a lot less violent.

At that point, the father, who had been sitting quietly, interrupted and gave me his version of what happened, which was quite different from what I'd heard from the son. "The other kid was really big. He came skating across the ice and just shoved my son into the glass," he told me. As he told it, the collision had been a major deal and his son had been badly shaken. I'd just heard two descriptions of the same play in which critical details were different.

This was my reading of the situation: The young man understood the seriousness of what had occurred. He'd had multiple concussions already, and in this case a relatively light blow to the head had caused some of those symptoms to return. That was a sign that his brain might be becoming more vulnerable. Continuing to play a collision sport such as hockey (he also played baseball) might be too risky.

The dad, on the other hand, wanted the kid to play again. It was a foregone conclusion that the young man had to sit out for a while because he was still experiencing concussion symptoms. But the dad was smart—he'd read up about treatment of concussions and sensed what I was listening for. Mild trauma that leads to severe concussion symptoms is a signal that the brain's defenses are declining. If I could establish that the blow had been a mild one, my opinion would be for that kid to never go back to the sport. So Dad preemptively jumped into the conversation to tell me, "I was there. I saw what happened to my son."

The young man had been *that* close to telling me, "Doc, I don't think I would have gotten these symptoms in the past." And his dad—a physician, by the way—had cut him off.

I looked over at the mom. She had been observing this scene from the corner of the room. She hadn't uttered a word, but her eyes and body language told me quite a bit about what she might have been thinking. She didn't seem happy.

I had just sat in on a little family drama. The parents were good, caring people. They obviously adored their son. But that morning in my office, the dad had fallen into a trap that many of us do.

He'd let passion for a child's sports life influence his decision-making as a parent. And as many of us do from time to time, he was making curious decisions. His son's future health was at stake, yet he was focused on protecting his status as a high school hockey player. Several months later, I saw the family again in the office. By then, the father's attitude had changed dramatically. He was sincerely appreciative that his son's concussion had been treated conservatively and that he had been kept out of harm's way.

The role of the physician is not to challenge a mom or dad. Parents have the right to raise their kids as they wish without unsolicited advice. I hope I am always respectful of that prerogative. Yet sometimes I do remind the patient and his parents that they have come to see me for my opinion and I assume they want all of it, not only the part that fits with their plans for the next few weeks or months. If a mom insists on her child going back to a cheerleading squad while she is experiencing concussion symptoms, I can't overrule that decision. I can — and I do — suggest that we should reconsider whether I am the best doctor for her child. Many doctors manage concussions well. It's important to find one the family is comfortable with. Most of my patients have been to several doctors and are coming to me willing and eager to listen. So these conversations are rare.

Infrequently, I am drawn into unspoken struggles between parent and child. Dad wants the child to play football, ice hockey, or another collision sport. The young man does not want to play. Concussion symptoms reported by the child are symptoms not of a concussion but of the conflict. During the first visit to my office, the kid learns that symptoms are a way out. As long as he has even one concussion symptom, he can't be cleared to go back to his sport. So he doesn't get better. Or if he does, he doesn't let on that his symptoms have disappeared. This can be a sign that a child is fearful of going back to the sport. In other cases, the child simply has developed new interests and wants to move on. The child's future playing football or lacrosse is so important to the parent that father and son can't have an honest conversation. Thus, an imagined injury is a way out.

These cases are easy to spot. Most kids can't wait to get back to their teams. Even before their symptoms lift, they're restless, wanting to get back in the weight room or back to practice. That is not the case with these patients. Playing is the last thing on their minds.

It's important to discuss what these athletes are really feeling and thinking, and to do so in a setting in which they feel safe. When their parents are out of the room, I will ask, "How much passion do you have for this sport?" "Whose idea was it to go out for the team?" "Are there sports you'd rather be playing?" "If so, why haven't you tried one?" I'm feathering around to find out whether the kid wants to play or if one parent is (or both parents are) making the call. Sometimes, a child isn't willing to open up and the conversation ends there. More often, kids want and need to talk.

Parents contribute so much to the sports lives of children, not only nursing them to health after a concussion but protecting them from injury. More can be done, and this is a good place to suggest areas where parent power is especially needed now.

Every high school in America should have a full-time athletic trainer. That would seem to be a given, a no-brainer. Yet according to recent data compiled by the National Athletic Trainers' Association, just 42 percent of high schools nationally have access to a trainer. In the 2010–11 school year, a record 7.7 million boys and girls participated in high school sports in the United States. According to that data, more than 4 million played an entire season without meeting an athletic trainer. Most state high school associations still do not require a trainer to be present at high school football games, an astonishing policy (or lack of one).

In Louisiana, the state legislature recently decided not to act on a proposal to require licensed trainers at junior high and high school football games. Supporters of the bill contended that it would prevent injuries and possibly deaths caused by head trauma. But the legislation failed when it was pointed out that it would add an expense to already underfunded school districts. Cost should be a factor, no doubt about it. But high school football jerseys, cleats, shoulder pads, and helmets are expensive, yet we find a way to pay for them.

Let's redouble our efforts to educate kids about concussions and to do it in a way that makes it clear that playing through an injury to the head or spinal cord is definitely not heroic.

ESPN conducted a survey of players, coaches, parents, and athletic trainers in twenty-three states. The sports network wanted to learn which group was least concerned about concussions. The winner was the group that should have been the most concerned — the players.

One of the survey questions dealt with a star player who'd suffered a concussion. The players were asked if they would rather lose a state title game because the star was forced to sit out or win it because he elected to play with a concussion. Fifty-four percent replied that they would play with the star. *Fifty-four percent.* That attitude has to change.

9

After Concussions

My advice is to not get too focused on sports. As long as you're healthy
and alive, you can do anything. The opportunities are endless.

— JAMES ORRIGO

S OME OF THE MOST difficult conversations I have with young
athletes who have prolonged post-concussion syndrome begin
with this thought: "It's time to stop playing your sport." Often the
message is harsher: "It's time to stop playing *all contact and collision
sports.*"

These meetings do not happen often, fortunately — sometimes
they're months apart. Yet they do happen, and for the kids involved,
the adjustment to life without a sport they love can be devastating.
Sports are at the center of their lives, connecting them with friends
and shaping how they see themselves.

When sports are yanked away, kids may stumble for a few weeks
or even months. It takes time for them to regain their balance.
Eventually, they dust themselves off and bounce back. Sometimes,
they roar back.

This chapter is about young athletes who roar. I want to tell you
about several inspiring patients and share their comeback stories.
For some, concussion symptoms still have not lifted, whereas others
recovered long ago. Each of these patients left my office with something precious missing from his or her life, yet turned the experience with head trauma into an opportunity, helping a lot of people
along the way.

Taylor Twellman

Until a few years ago, Taylor was one of the premier pro soccer players in the United States — a five-time all-star in Major League Soccer and the Most Valuable Player in the MLS in 2005. In eight years in the league, Taylor scored an impressive 101 goals. He was also a scoring threat during his time with the U.S. national team.

Taylor Twellman

Throughout his pro career, Taylor suffered concussions, five in all. The last occurred in 2008 in a game between the New England Revolution, Taylor's team, and the Los Angeles Galaxy. The collision that led to the concussion is one of the most violent I've seen in sports. Taylor was in the Galaxy goal crease, sprinting after a ball in the air. As Taylor's head was about to meet the ball, the Galaxy goalie reached out to punch it away and instead punched Taylor squarely in the face. As Taylor told me, "It was like running into a brick wall at a hundred miles per hour."

From what I have been told by others, including Taylor, little was done to check on him. The team trainer did a brief exam and cleared Taylor to return to the game. I'm not sure how that could happen, considering the condition Taylor was in. He reports now that he was seeing double. A few minutes later, he fired a shot ten feet to one side of the net. His vision and thinking were impaired to the point that he believed he had scored a goal and raised his arms in celebration.

Taylor played on for eight more games, scoring five more goals. That should not have happened either. When he came to my office for the first time, several months after the injury, he was rattled and demoralized. He had problems with memory and difficulty thinking clearly. Every morning he woke up with a searing headache.

For the next two years, Taylor waited for his symptoms to clear and clung to the hope that he would play again. I never met an athlete who worked harder at his recovery, or for whom getting back to his sport would have meant more. He told me, "The experience was extremely emotional. For months and months, there was not a twenty-four-hour period that I didn't break down and cry. On the really bad days, I cried all day. I tried everything, from acupuncture to sitting in a dark room for two months. Finally, I got to the point where I could work out for an hour a day. I started heading the ball at that point and everything got worse."

In 2010, Taylor announced his retirement at the age of thirty. His decision was national news, making headlines in *USA Today* and on ESPN. The end of his soccer career did not mean the end of Taylor's medical ordeal, however. The daily activities that we take for granted — and take pleasure in — made his symptoms worse. Reading, listening to music, even walking his dog seemed to amplify his headaches. "I miss my life, my old normal life," he said then.

Taylor began to throw himself into other endeavors. He was hired by ESPN as a soccer analyst, and now and then he told the story of his concussions. The head trauma discussion touched the audience. Parents started contacting Taylor. Their kids were going through similar hardships. His positive message — emphasizing education, awareness, putting the health of kids first — resonated with many.

A question sent to him by parents again and again concerned where to turn for medical care and advice. Taylor has strong feelings about this. For months after his concussion he'd bounced from doctor to doctor. Looking back, he realizes he should have seen a concussion specialist sooner. "With parents, the analogy I use is *If I break my foot, do I rush off to see an eye doctor?* No, I don't. I make an appointment with the orthopedic surgeon. The same reasoning goes into which doctor to go see with a concussion. Find someone who understands brains and brain injury."

After dispensing advice in this piecemeal fashion, Taylor started thinking bigger. That led to the launch of a charitable foundation and to a website, ThinkTaylor.org. Taylor's idea is simple — to use the soapbox that he has as a former athlete and broadcaster to educate families about head trauma.

Taylor has a thousand ideas about how to focus the influence and reach of ThinkTaylor.org. He wants to speak with youth soccer clubs as he travels around the country working for ESPN. He wants to get the word out by selling Think Taylor bracelets and shirts. (The Think Taylor T-shirt with a slick design is already for sale on the website.) He's hoping that his message will build a following of concerned fans who will become members of Think Taylor and support the foundation with small contributions. The money will be used for concussion research, he tells me.

"I look at what Lance Armstrong did for cancer research with Livestrong. It's a very high aspiration, I know. I'd like to do the same for kids and parents dealing with concussions. It may sound corny, but if a kid has a concussion I want to help."

T.J. Cooney

T.J. is an anomaly in this book. Of all the young athletes mentioned in these pages, T.J. is the only one who has not been my patient. But his story is so compelling, it bears telling here.

T.J. Cooney

T.J. played football at every level from the local youth leagues in his home state of New Jersey all the way up to the collegiate ranks at Catholic University in Washington, D.C. Football was always a major part of T.J.'s life. He loved everything about it — the competition, being part of a team, even the hitting. Especially the hitting. "For me, football was like a crutch," he explains. "When I was very young, my father left our family. Things at home were crazy for a while. Football was one of the consistent things in my life. It was something I did well and could never imagine giving up."

T.J. had little reason to think about concussions playing youth football and through his high school years. He remembers being raised to think that football players were tough, nearly indestructible. Of course, there were injuries that couldn't be played through. But not many, and they did not happen to the tough guys.

"Football players think that there are two different kinds of damage your body can take," he told me. "Being 'hurt' means you are in pain but can still play and can't get hurt any worse. Being 'injured' means that you cannot play, most likely because you have torn a ligament or broken a leg. Concussion for many years has floated between the two spectrums, and still does unfortunately. Which really leaves the severity of the injury up to the discretion of the athlete. For nearly my entire playing career, I thought extreme headaches were part of the game."

During T.J.'s sophomore season at Catholic University, he suffered a concussion during a practice. In a game nine days later, he suffered two more. The first happened on one of the last plays of the first half. As T.J. recalls, the hit left him with a severe headache. But he was a football player, and he was tough. He wasn't going to say anything about the head injury to his coaches or the athletic trainer. "It was one of the worst decisions I've ever made in my life," he said.

T.J. went back into the game in the second half and fell on his head. This time, he knew he was hurt badly. As T.J. tells it, that day began a journey filled with new and unwelcome challenges. The next morning, he could barely stand. His memory was severely impaired. There were other symptoms too — headaches and profound sleep problems.

T.J. spent the next eight months regaining control of his life. It turned out to be more difficult than he'd imagined. When he'd take sleep medications so that he could get a little rest, he'd wake up the next day so drowsy that he wasn't able to drag himself to class. That set off another round of problems. "I had been an A/B student. That semester my grades were awful. I couldn't remember anything."

Gradually, T.J.'s symptoms lifted. When football season at Catholic rolled around the next fall, T.J. had a goal — returning to the team. When practices began, T.J. was on the field. "Before they started, I told myself, *If you have an inkling that things aren't going well, stop. Just stop.* I'd gone through the worst year of my life. I was thankful just to have my sanity back."

For two weeks, all went well. Then in a practice drill, T.J. made a tackle. He threw off his helmet and walked off the field. His eyes hurt and other old concussion symptoms had returned.

That was T.J.'s last day as a football player. To this day he deals with the loss of something that was a huge part of his life.

"I think about football all the time. It taught me a lot of life lessons. Such as, when you get knocked down, you've got to get back up. The cliché things in life that are true. I would give my left hand to play again. But I can't, and I've had to come to terms with that. It is what it is. I love that I had all those years playing football, but I don't reminisce about my past. Maybe because I don't remember."

Without football, T.J. felt rudderless. He compensated by throwing his energy into school, and particularly a class on filmmaking. He had always had ambitions to be a filmmaker, or at least to experiment with expressing his ideas on film. A major assignment for the semester was to create a short documentary. Students were encouraged to choose a subject that meant a lot to them and perhaps that they had personal experience with.

T.J. didn't hesitate. From the moment he learned of the assignment, he knew his documentary would deal with sports concussions. The film is titled *The Silent Epidemic.* T.J. thought that was fitting, given the stealth nature of the injury and the lack of understanding about what head trauma is and is not.

He carefully crafted a story line and chose several subjects to interview. They include two youth athletes who'd suffered concussions. One is a fellow football player from Catholic. Another is a former ice hockey player who quit the sport rather than face a lifetime of health problems. That interview is particularly affecting as the young man explains, "My hands shook for a while." Speaking of his life now, he adds, "Mornings are worst for me. It takes me a while to shake off all the symptoms." Another interview is with Dr. Michael Yochelson, medical director for the brain injury programs and associate medical director for neurological programs at National Rehabilitation Hospital in Washington, D.C., and the concussion specialist who had stood by T.J. during his recovery.

T.J. put one other eyewitness to sports concussions into his documentary. He interviewed himself. The recurring theme of the documentary is a simple one, and an important one: "It's better to sit out a game than sit out your whole life."

Dylan Mello

Dylan has already appeared in this book. As described in the chapter on post-concussion syndrome, Dylan's life playing ice hockey and soccer was derailed by a series of concussions, including a final one that — and Dylan would be the first to agree — could have been avoided. Dylan was playing in a summer soccer tournament in Maine. A player on the opposing soccer team arrived at the game in uniform, wearing a hard cast on his arm. There apparently were no rules preventing players from participating with a cast, though for

Dylan Mello

safety reasons it seems obvious that there should have been. Dylan and the opposing player were pursuing the ball when they collided. The hard cast banged against Dylan's head, leaving a scrape across his face.

That collision contributed to post-concussion syndrome, one of the more severe cases I have seen in recent years. Dylan was forced to give up all sports. On my recommendation, he delayed his freshman year of college one full year. He still has symptoms — a reminder that he is still recovering. Yet Dylan has turned these challenges into an opportunity to lobby for more stringent concussion laws.

Dylan lives in Rhode Island, a state so small that, as he's explained to me, everybody knows everybody else. As a talented athlete who'd gotten publicity for his great play, he already had a small dose of celebrity. Dylan's role as a citizen advocate added to that.

In 2010, the Rhode Island state legislature opened hearings on a bill regarding care of athletes who like Dylan slam their heads. The state delegate Raymond Gallison, who represented the Mellos' hometown of Portsmouth, sponsored the bill. Among its requirements is that kids who suffer head trauma receive written clearance from a licensed healthcare professional with training in treating concussions before they are permitted back in the game.

The hearing received considerable attention. Several TV stations in Providence, the state capital, interviewed Dylan. Newspapers reported on the hearing too. The next day's *Providence Journal* carried articles and Web video of Dylan telling his story to legislators and explaining that he hoped to educate others and to spare kids from injuries like those he had suffered.

Dylan told the legislators that his recovery had been complicated by a series of mistakes and oversights. Initially, he'd been treated by a family doctor. He would have been better off in the care of a physician with training in head trauma. He played for weeks with a headache and other concussion symptoms, which he'd concealed from his parents and coaches. Looking back, Dylan said, it was shortsighted not to have been truthful. "I feel my injuries in part are due to my own ignorance and stubbornness," Dylan said. He explained that the effects of his concussions were with him every day. "I have trouble in school. I need extra time on tests. I can't run, or do cardio. I can't watch TV. I feel that for the past year I have been trapped inside my own body."

Dylan concluded by telling the committee members, "I don't want anyone to go through what I have gone through."

If there was any question about the force and impact of Dylan's testimony, it was answered six months later when the concussion bill passed the state legislature and became law. Dylan acknowledged that being at the center of the concussion debate in his home state hadn't been completely comfortable. "I wasn't one hundred percent for it," he said. "There were days I told my mom I just couldn't stand up in front of people and discuss it anymore. At times, it felt like I was the poster boy for concussions. I never wanted to be the kid that became infamous for a head injury. On the other hand, there were positives. In a small way, maybe I helped get the law passed."

Alyssa Blood

A few years ago, I had one of those "I know you love basketball . . . but" conversations with Alyssa. It ended with me counseling — and Alyssa agreeing — that her days as a competitive athlete had come to an end. At the time, she was starting her senior year of college. She had suffered four concussions in three different sports. The final concussion had been the worst, sidelining her for nearly two years.

Alyssa's health issues had interrupted a promising basketball career at Brown University. She came to the school with loads of potential and the height (six foot one) to be a top rebounder in the Ivy League. Alyssa never had a chance to become the player she might have been. As a freshman, she suffered a concussion on the court and was out for five weeks. She made a complete recovery only to have a concussion the next season. She was working toward yet another comeback; during a trip home to England she joined a United Kingdom twenty-and-under national team. Her symptoms returned, and to her frustration she was sidelined again.

Alyssa Blood

Even then Alyssa hadn't given up on her basketball dream. When I saw her in my office in October 2010, she was a senior at Brown, contemplating a return to the Bears for one last season. That summer she had worked diligently at getting into the best shape possible — lifting weights and pushing through cardio workouts, doing everything a college basketball player would do except play college basketball.

She came to my office for what she described as a "signoff" visit, expecting to receive permission to begin preparing for the season. Alyssa remembers arriving with her parents and explaining her plans. She clearly recalls my reaction if not the exact words. It was something like "Are you kidding? You've been sick for two years."

I hope I was more diplomatic. I was firm with Alyssa and her parents that day in my office. Playing again was not an option I could recommend. The risk of yet another concussion — and even more severe symptoms — was too great.

"It was not a negotiation," Alyssa says now. "I remember leaving the office feeling weird. For the first time I could remember, there was nothing to train for. No season to point at. I remember exactly how I responded. I went home and went for a twelve-mile run."

Even though Alyssa had been absent from the Brown team for a long stretch, she had believed that she would be able to return. Accepting reality took several months. "I don't think anyone is well prepared for that dramatic a change in your life. I was blinded by what I wanted and by my goals. I'd worked hard to become the best basketball player I could be. It took time to realize that in the long term, that's not as important as having high cognitive ability for the rest of your life."

Eventually, Alyssa even forgave me for our honest conversation that day in my office.

"At the moment, it may seem that doctors are out there to prevent you from doing the things you love just so they can make you miserable." She breaks into a big smile and adds, "I don't think that's true."

Without basketball in her life, Alyssa channeled her ambition in new directions. Though she wasn't able to continue playing at the most competitive levels of sports, she didn't have to stop being active. She became interested in yoga and picked up tennis, a sport that she had excelled at in high school. Eventually she even got back to the gym for occasional pickup basketball games — noncontact and very casual.

Alyssa also began to see her concussions in a different light: as an experience, even a teaching moment. Alyssa and I were invited to speak at a colloquium at Brown on the danger of concussions in sports. Alyssa was poised and impressive, telling her story and explaining that concussions can occur in all sports — not football and ice hockey exclusively. Several parents and coaches approached after the program that night, seeking her advice for their families or others they knew. A few months later a producer for a TV show called and asked if I could recommend a patient for an interview.

Alyssa was featured on a report about concussions in youth sports on *Today*, NBC's popular morning show. That brought a new wave of attention and more e-mails and calls.

"It's flattering to be thought of as an expert," she says of her newfound status. "Sometimes I had to stop and say, 'Hey, guys, I'm not a doc.'"

Until this time, Alyssa's career goals had been to work on Wall Street or perhaps in politics. Those options began to seem less attractive than a career in medicine, helping other head trauma victims. She set out on a new path to become a neurologist.

"As I was recovering from my concussions, I became very interested in what was going on with my body. More than anything, I wanted to be normal and deal with normal people problems," she said. "I was tired of being sick all the time. I realized there are so many people coping with the same issues."

After graduating from Brown in 2011, Alyssa enrolled at Georgetown University, where she took the pre-med courses she needed before applying to medical school. In her spare hours she worked at a pediatric concussion clinic in Washington, D.C. She said the experience was valuable — she was able to see head trauma from the perspective of an intern working with patients rather than as a patient coping with symptoms.

Initially Alyssa's ordeal seemed to change her life in all the wrong ways. As she looks back now, she believes the experience gave her purpose and direction. "It's a cliché, but things really do happen for a reason," she told me. "I was looking for something to inspire me and I found it."

James Orrigo

I'm not offering many music reviews in this book, despite loving music and playing currently in the Yankee Stompers, a Dixieland jazz band, and the Colonial Jazz, a jazz quintet. But I do have one review. The next time you are in front of your computer, go to a digital music Web site and type this name into the search engine: James

James Orrigo

Orrigo. That will lead you to *Coming Home,* an album released in November 2011. Now click on a song from the album that is silly and profound and will stay with you for a long time: "Boat Shoes." (Plan B: Watch a performance on YouTube.)

I met James when he was sixteen years old. In 2007, he came to my office suffering from post-concussion syndrome. James reported eleven different concussion symptoms that day, nervousness, poor memory, fatigue, drowsiness, and a moderate headache among them.

James had suffered two concussions in succession during a high school lacrosse game. Before his head injury, he'd been an upbeat and optimistic person. The symptoms had worn him down, though. He hadn't been able to return to lacrosse. His schoolwork was suffering. He'd been a high-achieving student. But since the concussions, no amount of studying had been enough. When he sat down to take the exam, the information was lost.

James's recovery from post-concussion syndrome was lengthy and at times discouraging. It took nearly two years for his brain to heal. Meanwhile, he went through periods in which improvement was slow, almost invisible. He wondered whether he would ever be well. James's mother saw her son's helplessness and decided to do something. As James tells it, "She didn't want me sitting around feeling depressed. One of our neighbors played the guitar. She asked if he would come over and teach me. It came easily. I learned in two weeks." He smiles and adds, "Maybe the concussions had something to do with it."

Music wasn't the only challenge and opportunity in James's life. About this time, he was asked to speak at a school assembly about his struggle with concussions. He was reluctant — he was still suffering from headaches and he stuttered a bit, an effect of the head trauma. But he agreed and enjoyed talking about all he had been through. There were more invitations and more speeches. Over the next several months, James spoke at more than a half dozen forums on sports concussions, sharing his experiences. I used James for many of the concussion talks I gave at local high schools, and while the parents might have heard some of what I said, the athletes and students only had ears for James.

The speeches were a prelude to James's stepping onto a larger stage. After high school, he enrolled at James Madison University, where few students knew him as the kid who suffered concussions playing sports. He had an entirely different identity on campus. He was James Orrigo the musician and performer.

In his first two years at JMU, James wrote sixty-one songs. He performed for friends and entered campus talent shows. As a freshman, he won the Madison Idol competition, a local version of *American Idol*. His winning performance was "Boat Shoes."

"Most of my songs are fun and happy-go-lucky. If I can make people smile and have a good time, I've accomplished something important," he said.

Not all of his songs are lighthearted. For several years, he has been working on a song called "Concussion Blues." When I asked about it, hoping to hear a few bars, he told me, "It isn't really a song. I've never written it down. It's just something I was messing around with one night, and my mother had a video camera." The first words: "There's this brain injury called a concussion."

James is more than a musician and songwriter. He also is a social activist with a strong conviction that we all ought to be giving back to people in our communities. As I said, he's an exceptional person. Several years ago, he created an alter ego that he calls Lad in a Battle. "Lad" is an acronym for Life Above Alcohol and Drugs, a philosophy that James lives by and espouses to his friends and fans. He doesn't drink or smoke. He's unfailingly polite. He hasn't had a bad day since his concussion symptoms disappeared a few years ago. That's the feeling you have hanging around with James Orrigo.

"In a Battle" refers to a mission that James is on to encourage his friends and followers to embrace public service. In a sense, he is leading a good-deeds movement. He encourages his fans to commit a selfless act each day — something as simple as helping an elderly person cross the street or picking up litter in their neighborhoods. His followers are easy to spot. Many wear Lad in a Battle T-shirts that James had printed up to galvanize his group — and to raise money for charity. (Proceeds from T-shirt sales go to the Make-A-Wish Foundation.)

James is spreading his message throughout the country. A few years ago, he planned a Lad in a Battle Tour. After his final exams at James Madison, he traveled from Virginia to Maine, performing and delivering motivational talks at high schools. There was no staging or backup band. Just James under a spotlight with his guitar and his message. He visited dozens of schools along the route. "It was a great experience. Everywhere I went, I spoke about how you can do anything you want to do. The kids opened up so much to that message."

10

Reforms

There's a lot of parents who have such high expectations and such hopes for their kid's success in athletic competition that they don't want them to come off the field.

— REP. GEORGE MILLER, D-California (*San Jose Mercury News*)

SPORTS FANS TYPICALLY have favorite athletes that they root for and admire from a distance. I admit to having a favorite parent of an athlete. It's a little different, but consider the story of Tom Brady Sr.

Tom and his wife, Galynn, have four children, three daughters and the baby of the Brady clan, Tom Jr. These days, Tom Jr. is the quarterback of the New England Patriots and widely thought to be the best quarterback of his generation if not all time. If they could find it on a store shelf, millions of American dads and moms would pay for the formula that the Bradys used to raise one of the best quarterbacks ever.

Recently, I had an opportunity to speak with Tom Sr. about kids, sports, and safety. We met in my office for an hour and then continued the conversation at a charity function in Boston that we both happened to be attending. Tom told me about his son's background in youth football. I found the story important and compelling for parents with kids not only in football but in other sports.

Youth football programs were plentiful in San Mateo, California, when Tom Brady was growing up in the late 1980s and early '90s. Within ten minutes of the Bradys' front door, they had their choice of leagues for their son to play in when he was six or eight or twelve. Yet the Bradys elected not to sign up their son. Instead, Tom Jr. played pickup football in the street in front of the Bradys' home. His parents were removed from the picture entirely. "The first time I ever saw Tommy seriously throw a football, he was fourteen years of age," Tom Sr. told me. Tom Jr., perhaps the most outstanding quarterback of our time, did not play organized football until his freshman year at Junipero Serra High School. Even that year, he did not make it into a game for a single play.

In the 1980s, few physicians were talking about concussions in youth sports. Even fewer parents were concerned. Why would the Bradys hold back a son whose athletic talent was so evident? "For a child that age, football is too rough. As a parent, I didn't want my seven- or eight-year-old kid walking off the field with a broken arm or leg," Tom Sr. told me. "Frankly, I think it's almost child abuse."

The story of the Brady clan focuses attention on what's important about youth sports and what's important to change. This final chapter offers a road map of sorts, a way forward that embraces the fun and good times that sports for kids offer at the same time that it lowers the threat of head trauma.

No tackle football before fourteen.

It's telling that some of the adults with the greatest fears about tackle football are those who earned their living playing it.

The former NFL quarterback Troy Aikman suffered ten concussions — those are the ones he knew about — during his Hall of Fame career with the Dallas Cowboys. In 2010, Aikman told HBO's Bryant Gumbel, "I think that we're at a real crossroads, as it relates to the grassroots of our sport, because if I had a ten-year-old boy, I don't know that I'd be real inclined to encourage him to go play football, in light of what we are learning from head injury."

Other NFL players, past and present, are similarly ambivalent. Not long ago, I had a conversation with Jeff Saturday, the Indianapolis Colts center who all these years has been hiking the ball through his legs to the Hall of Famer Peyton Manning. Jeff told me point-blank that his son, Jeffrey, won't play youth football. Too dangerous.

The issue has special poignancy for the family of Tom McHale, a former Cornell University and NFL lineman. In 2008, Tom died of a drug overdose after a battle with prescription medications. He'd gotten hooked on the painkillers that he'd used to dull the pain from football injuries. Tom's wife, Lisa, donated her husband's brain to our brain bank at the Bedford Veterans Administration Medical Center. The autopsy revealed CTE, a signal that brain trauma had contributed to Tom's death at age forty-five.

In 2010, the ESPN reporter Tom Farrey spoke with Lisa McHale about her children. At the time, one of her sons was playing lacrosse and another was a tennis player. Lisa would not permit either to play tackle football. "For my kids," she told Farrey, "I can't take that risk."

Ideally, tackle football for kids would begin at fourteen, the age when most kids are entering high school and trying out for the team with their classroom buddies. Admittedly, the number is not set in stone. Like most mandatory minimums and maximums ("Ten items or less"), it is arbitrary to a degree. However, the age of fourteen correlates with the development of our bodies' natural protections against head trauma. By age fourteen, our necks are strong and our overall body strength is sufficient to keep the head steady (or steadier) when slammed at the line of scrimmage. Brains have matured too, and developed a protective myelin coating.

Kids can make their own choices at fourteen. This is as much an ethical as a medical consideration, and important for parents to think about. A teenager entering high school, if he is the child we have raised him to be, can make a reasoned judgment about the risks and rewards of playing tackle football. A teen won't weigh these factors as a parent would. But he has the capacity to think for himself. The same is not true of six-year-olds, of course. Each time that child puts on shoulder pads, he is assuming a risk that he isn't old enough to understand. It may be that the child in years to come will be grateful to his parents for putting him in tackle football — or maybe not.

Will we ever be able to shut the spigot of youth football? Will the parents and other supervising adults responsible for those three million children ages six to fourteen playing in organized leagues ever conclude that the safe and smart thing to do is wait until high school? Even for neurosurgeons and other optimists, that seems doubtful. The sport is just too entrenched. Kids want to play tackle football. More important, their parents want them to play too. There has to be a Plan B.

Mine is a multipart approach emphasizing education and a significant reduction in contact, both during preseason and in-season workouts. Education efforts should move forward on all fronts so that parents, coaches, and children appreciate that head trauma is in a category all its own. You can gut it out and play with a big bruise or hip flexor. There is never a scenario in which playing with a head or spinal injury, or a suspicion of such an injury, should be condoned.

Several clever education programs aim at the important issue of encouraging children to report their symptoms to a coach or parent. None impresses me more than the concussion education messages now contained in the Madden Football video games. In 2011, the creators of the Madden franchise, EA Sports, changed course with their depiction of concussions. For the first time, when a virtual player in the game had a concussion, that player was ruled out for the rest of that game. The gaming company also eliminated all depictions of helmet-to-helmet hits out of concern that what kids see on their screens is behavior they will model when they are in pads.

"Concussions are such a big, big thing, it has to be a big thing in the video game," John Madden, the game's namesake and a former NFL coach, said of the new features in the *New York Times*.

It's only logical that video gaming would be an effective method for educating kids about concussions and to impress on them the importance of coming forward with symptoms they are feeling and otherwise might ignore. There's also confirmation in research just now beginning about sports, gaming, and head trauma education. One such study led by David Goodman of Simon Fraser University in Canada involved creating a rudimentary computer hockey game in which messages about concussions were embedded. Youth hockey players, between the ages of eleven and seventeen, who'd played the game consistently scored higher in a test in which they were tasked with recognizing concussion symptoms than those who hadn't. And they wanted to play the games again.

Education is only part of the answer. A comprehensive approach to reducing head trauma also must include a significant reduction in the number of hits in youth football. This is needed at all levels and especially high school football. The most important step is a profound rethinking of practice. Many high school teams work out nearly every day. During preseason the schedule can be nearly every day, twice a day. Practices are when and where most of the head trauma in football occurs. For that reason, it's where a lot could be eliminated. No doubt, some purists would complain that the sport was being changed for the worse. I can hear them now: With fewer crunching tackles and helmet-on-helmet hits, football just wouldn't be football. In reply, I'd point to an octogenarian Hall of Fame coach whose no-tackle practices prove that's just a lot of bunk. Right, John Gagliardi?

Helmets aren't the solution to the head trauma crisis in football. They never will be the solution in football. Helmets provide excellent protection against concussions in some sports, those in which head trauma mostly is caused by linear forces — a hard slam to the helmet with a stick or a ball. Concussions in football often are the result of rotational forces — a crunching tackle that jerks the head from side to side in a whiplash effect. Helmets are nearly worthless as protection against hits such as that.

I am vice president of the National Operating Committee on Standards for Athletic Equipment (NOCSAE), the national organization in the lead on setting safety standards for athletic equipment. I also serve the organization as chair of a committee that advises the board on matters of science. NOCSAE is impressive because it brings together equipment manufacturers, athletic trainers, coaches, and doctors to spur research for safer equipment in all sports. In 2011, NOCSAE awarded more than $1 million in research grants to study football-helmet standards.

Without doubt, helmets will improve over time. Will helmets ever prevent concussions in football? For that to occur, the manufacturers would have to do a lot more than tweak the design. They'd have to overcome the laws of physics.

A story told to me by T.J. Cooney underscores the point. When he played football for Catholic University, T.J. went out and bought the most expensive helmet on the market. He believed a helmet that made all sorts of claims about cutting-edge technology would limit his exposure to head trauma. On the first day of fall practice, he was hit in the head and suffered a concussion that ended his career. "Ironically," he says, "the worst concussion of my life happened while I was wearing the best helmet out there."

No body checking in youth hockey before age fourteen.

Applause to USA Hockey and Hockey Canada. These youth sports organizations deserve recognition for taking steps to reduce hitting in youth hockey. They shouldn't get complacent. I say finish the job and impose a ban on body checking until the age of fourteen.

What I propose is more complicated than it sounds. I understand that. Currently, USA Hockey has a Peewees division for players ages eleven and twelve, and a Bantams division for players thirteen and fourteen. The Bantams would have a problem if the rules allowed body checking for only half the players. How those structural changes are worked out is a matter for officials who live and breathe youth hockey and not for me to say. However, we all can agree that the safety of the players must come first.

The National Hockey League should take a long look in the mirror. Violence at NHL arenas continues to be tolerated, even glorified. That's dangerous for players and sends a confusing message to kids who live to shoot the puck. It's alarming that the NHL would continue to drag its feet on true rules reform when the plight of former NHL players stricken with degenerative brain disease has become part of the daily sports discussion. In December 2011, John Branch of the *New York Times* wrote a three-part series on the life and death of the NHL bruiser Derek Boogaard titled "Punch Out: The Life and Death of a Hockey Enforcer." Boogaard died of a lethal mix of alcohol and the prescription drug oxycodone, according to a medical examiner's report. Boogaard's brain was donated to our brain bank, where Dr. McKee confirmed that he had CTE. It hadn't killed Boogaard, but had he lived another thirty years, the typical progression of the disease might have. When he died, Boogaard was twenty-eight.

That tragic story could have been a call to action for the NHL, but the opportunity was missed. The same week, the commissioner Gary Bettman told the *Times*, "Our fans tell us they like the physicality in our game," as if catering to a ticket buyer's taste for on-ice brawling is more important than protecting the league's own players. It was a weak and baffling response.

Until the NHL acts, a suggestion from Don Cherry, a former NHL coach and now TV commentator, may be the best we can hope for. Don recommends that NHL players wear helmets stamped with the league's seldom enforced policy on intentional blows. Each helmet would have a one-word admonition on the front: S-T-O-P.

Helmets should be required in field hockey and girls' lacrosse.

Helmets eventually will be mandatory in these two sports. There are too many girls suffering facial and brain injuries and preventable skull fractures for this not to happen in five years or, at the outside, ten. So why not get on with it?

For now, the national governing bodies of these sports oppose any such requirements. An objection frequently voiced is that making helmets mandatory for girls will cause the sports to become more dangerous, not less. Steve Stenersen, president and CEO of U.S. Lacrosse, explained it this way: "We don't think the women's game should become a collision sport."

Unlike most sports played by boys and girls, the rules of lacrosse differ substantially by gender. In the boys' game, contact between players is permitted. In the girls' game, it isn't. Boys wear helmets covering the head with attached facemasks. Girls do not wear helmets. However, they are required to wear goggles for eye protection and mouth guards to shield their teeth and gums.

Steve and I agree completely that changes to girls' lacrosse should not make the sport more physical. We disagree about what is needed to protect the young women playing the sport now.

I believe in a substantial helmet for the girls. It should cover the head completely and be lightweight so as not to impede movement from side to side. It should also be designed to ensure that girls maintain a clear field of vision. These are readily achievable goals. With the technology available today, every young woman could be wearing a helmet like the one just described. (Goalies already do.)

Steve tells me that U.S. Lacrosse supports a modified helmet for girls, one that would cover the top of the head and look somewhat like a bicycle helmet. U.S. Lacrosse deserves credit for having a helmet proposal. This suggestion is inadequate, however. That isn't only my opinion. It's the opinion of NOCSAE, the aforementioned organization that sets safety standards for sports equipment. NOCSAE has tested helmets like those being suggested by U.S. Lacrosse. The results weren't encouraging. These models tested poorly for protection against concussion-type hits. In reply to U.S. Lacrosse, NOCSAE said, in effect, if there are going to be helmets for girls, they should be equivalent in protection to the guys' helmets. Nothing less.

The value of helmets in women's lacrosse is well known to Kristen Chapman. Kristen plays midfield for Yale University. Kristen suffered two concussions in just ten months. The first occurred when

Kristen Chapman

she was slammed over the head with a stick and the second while she was working at a sports camp and banged her head on cement. Kristen was sidelined for months and became understandably impatient.

Eventually, Kristen's symptoms cleared and we began to discuss whether it was prudent for her to return to her sport. As her doctor, I had concerns about her concussion history and the potential for another head injury.

We agreed that she could return to the Yale team if she wore a helmet. Initially, Kristen wore a modified ice hockey helmet with the facemask removed and extra padding packed across the top. It wasn't perfect—it was heavy and bulky and at times impeded her line of sight. It got her back in the game, though. She returned the following spring wearing a helmet that she made from a bike helmet. What followed was both unfortunate and instructive. Wearing the minimalist helmet, Kristen suffered yet another concussion and was back in recovery mode.

Boys' lacrosse also has work to do, particularly in protecting the youngest players from head trauma. It is long past time that intentional contact between players be taken out of the game until age fourteen. Accidents happen, of course. And in a sport as fast-paced as lacrosse — with players changing direction constantly — only so much contact can be eliminated. But the intentional stuff should stop until the players — as in football and hockey — turn fourteen.

Field hockey helmets are a necessary idea for the same reasons that helmets in girls' lacrosse are. Without them, the players are too vulnerable. The rules state that players should not bring sticks above the knee. It happens in every game, of course. When it does, players sometimes suffer concussions, eye injuries, lacerations, broken noses, and more. Field hockey players should be required to wear a helmet with a mask. End of discussion. Does the helmet have to be as robust as a boys' football helmet? No. Is there any need to have the same discussion five years from now? Also no.

No heading in soccer until fourteen.

We can't say whether heading a soccer ball over and over for many years increases a person's risk of one day developing CTE. No studies that I am aware of have made this connection. In fact, there aren't any studies that I would rely on linking cleanly heading the ball — the act of head meeting ball with no other trauma to the head — with a higher rate of severe brain injury.

We can say with authority that if heading simply vanished from youth soccer the sport would go from being risky from the standpoint of head trauma to one of the safest. So much happens when a young player springs into the air expecting to meet the ball with her forehead, and so much of it results in head trauma. Head meeting ball is the scenario of least concern. Problems arise when head meets shoulder, elbow, or another head.

Those who favor heading maintain that it's a big part of the sport and that removing it from soccer would deprive children of the chance to develop as players. I don't agree. Neither does Taylor

Twellman, whose pro soccer career was cut short by post-concussion syndrome. "Does anything change if we eliminate heading in soccer before high school?" he says. "Nothing changes at all."

Taylor describes going to a youth practice and watching coaches working on heading, kicking balls in the air and sending them down on seven- or eight-year-old heads. Each kid is served up twenty or more balls in a single workout. "It doesn't make sense to me," Taylor says. "How about waiting until their brains are more fully developed at thirteen or fourteen?"

I have to admit that not all coaches and parents are rallying around a ban on heading for kids. Still, there are clubs and rec leagues around the country that like the idea, including the Pine Bush Youth Soccer Club in Pine Bush, New York (population: 1,780). In this progressive little club, heading is not permitted for second- and third-graders. For fourth- and fifth-graders, heading is permitted but, according to club rules, "not encouraged." There are many other clubs and rec leagues implementing such rules. The tide finally may be turning.

Hold sports officials to a higher standard.

Officiating games at the youth sports level is a difficult job. High school officials are perpetually in short supply because the pay is so low and the behavior of fans and coaches is such a turnoff. Recently, the *New York Times* quoted a basketball official who'd decided to hang up his whistle after thirty years because he was weary of the abuse. "It gets old night after night," he told the *Times,* noting that he preferred the serenity of his full-time job as a firefighter.

As appreciative as most of us are of these officials and the jobs they do, they're not above criticism that's offered constructively. During games, officials are the only adults on the field or the ice. We depend on them to enforce the rules. A lacrosse stick across the head is illegal and should be called a penalty. A blind-side hit to the head in hockey is illegal and should be called a penalty. When players flout the rules, officials must call penalties. When they don't, youth players become emboldened and go after the next kid more recklessly than the last.

Several national organizations do a good job providing educational programs and other support for the tens of thousands of amateur officials working in high school gyms and on neighborhood rec fields. The National Federation of State High School Associations (NFHS), the umbrella organization for high school sports in the United States, recently urged a "renewed emphasis" by officials to crack down on illegal hits in football. The NFHS implored officials to call penalties for helmet-to-helmet contact and slaps to the head by defenders, as well as infractions for unnecessary roughness.

That's a good start. Now game officials must be held accountable for the calls they make and, importantly, do not make. Every referee will miss a call or two — that's normal and part of the game. When dangerous plays are overlooked repeatedly, there need to be consequences. That official needs someone to tap him on the shoulder and say, "Hey, these are kids. Let's protect them." Perhaps underperforming referees ought to lose a paycheck or serve a suspension of several weeks. Officials with long experience in youth sports no doubt would come up with a much better system than an interloper like me. The point is that there needs to be a system.

Ironically, a sport we can hold up as a model for exemplary officiating is boxing (ironically because from the perspective of head trauma, it's the only thing about boxing that I'd hold up as a model). In boxing, the referee's responsibility in the ring is to protect the fighters from each other and from themselves. If the fighters hit below the belt or rabbit punch (behind the head), he tells them to stop. If a fighter is knocked to the canvas, the referee immediately sends the fighter still on his feet to an opposite corner — to protect the injured fighter. If a fighter is cut or hurt or incapable of defending himself, the responsibility to stop the fight again rests with the referee. Boxing referees I have known understand this aspect of the job and have fulfilled the responsibility faithfully. Maybe the answer is to train football officials to think more like boxing referees.

The NFL is once again setting the standard. Recently, the league began allowing referees that suspected an athlete of having signs of a head injury to send that player to the sidelines to be checked out. Similarly, the same call can be made by an official placed in a box high above the field.

For youth baseball, require chin straps and restrict the headfirst slide.

Batting helmets are mandatory at every level of baseball. They're such a part of youth baseball that if a kid walks up to home plate without a helmet on her head, the umpire, coaches in both dugouts, and every adult on the bleachers yells out to her to go back to the dugout and put a helmet on. Considering all that, it's surprising how little we do to ensure that the batting helmets we put on kids' heads stay on their heads, especially when all that's required is a chin strap. The importance of helmets staying put when kids are running the bases can't be overstated. Some youth leagues around the country have mandated chin straps for many years. That all youth and high school leagues have not is insane to me.

Headfirst slides are risky from the standpoint of head and cervical spine trauma. At the youth level, they should be banned — the headfirst slide to the next base and the headfirst slide back to the base from which the runner is coming. Too many things — all with the potential to rattle the brain or break the neck and cause paralysis — can happen when the runner leads with his head. There's a possibility that the baseball and the head will arrive at the same place at the same time, with serious consequences. There's also the risk to the head and neck from making abrupt impact with the fielder's foot or leg. If that isn't reason enough, there's one more. Sliding headfirst gets your shirt dirty.

Everyone, calm down.

Sports for kids are a wonderful thing, and I hope nothing I have written thus far suggests otherwise. Sports promote important values for children, the future Hall-of-Famers and those whose talents will not take them quite as far. There is nothing like being part of a Little League team or competing as a swimmer, tennis player, or golfer to promote perseverance, sportsmanship, fair play, and the value of fighting until the last point in the match or the last out. These are traits that carry us through the challenges we face in life.

I am concerned about the direction of youth sports, however. Over the past twenty years or so, it's all become so serious. Fun no longer seems to be the main object. Now it seems to be about grooming your child to be a star. It can be taken to extremes, such as sports training for babies and infants. As the *New York Times* reported, one youth fitness entrepreneur in Michigan has started a company that produces workout DVDs for children before they're even a year old. One of the exercises featured resembles batting practice for babies. While a parent gently holds them, kids grip a paper towel holder and swing at a balloon.

Most of the parents we see in our office have perspective about their children's sports lives. But there are also moms and dads who lose track of what's important. Recently, a mother came to the office with her daughter, a cheerleader who had fallen during a routine. She suffered a concussion and had several symptoms, including a headache that lingered a month or so. My advice was to limit activity and that she not go back to her cheerleading team until all symptoms had disappeared.

I wanted to see her again in about six weeks, as I normally would with a patient under such circumstances. The mom was unhappy that we wouldn't be meeting again sooner and reacted quite negatively. "She can't wait that long. She's missing the entire cheerleading season."

The mother's focus was on her daughter's status with the team, which she apparently saw slipping away. It seemed she hadn't considered the risks involved in going back to the team (though we had discussed them at length during the appointment). If she was thinking about another concussion and how seriously that might injure her daughter, she'd pushed that from her mind too.

There's a belief that the younger we start our kids in sports and the more training we drill into them, the better off they'll be. The facts simply don't support that. The early birds will have an edge for a while from the first-rate coaching and heavy doses of practicing and playing, but the advantage won't last. Ultimately, kids will reach their level of excellence based largely on genetic potential. Rushing them back from an injury jeopardizes even that possibility.

In my meeting with Tom Brady Sr., we chatted about his children and the goals he had for them in sports and other activities. He explained that he and his wife had allowed their children to take the lead in pursuing their interests. No one was forced or even coaxed. "In our family, the kids played the sports they wanted to play. My wife and I got to live our lives. We didn't get to live our lives through our children," he told me.

Maureen, the oldest of three sisters, was a star softball pitcher at Fresno State. Julie, the Brady's middle daughter, was a walk-on soccer player at St. Mary's College before earning a scholarship. Nancy, the youngest, landed a roster spot on the highly competitive softball team at Cal-Berkeley. She decided she'd had enough and left the team during her first season, with the full support of her parents.

As for Tom Jr., his dad explained that the star quarterback we know today was too busy excelling at other sports to worry about the one that his parents would not allow him to play. Tom Sr. says that one of the wisest parenting decisions he and his wife made was to hold their son out of tackle football until he reached high school. In light of what we now know about the risks, he wonders why more parents do not agree. "To put a kid out there at the age of nine or ten, it doesn't make any darn sense."

Postscript

When I began thinking about this book and what might be accomplished by writing it, I kept returning to one thought. Actually, one thought in four bullet points. If readers took away these four points, used them in caring for their children, and shared them with others they knew whose children play sports, the book would be a success. They're found throughout these pages, and I'll take the opportunity to repeat them here at the end.

- Educate kids, parents, and coaches about the fact that it's never safe to play with symptoms of a concussion.
- The best therapy we have for treating concussion symptoms is cognitive and physical rest.
- When a concussion is managed properly, the patient will get better.
- When a concussion isn't managed well, the patient runs a significant risk of lengthening the period of his or her symptoms and possibly developing post-concussion syndrome. In a few tragic cases, the patient can suffer second impact syndrome and die.

There is much more to know and to incorporate into caring for a child with a concussion, of course. These points are a good foundation. In virtually all cases, they'll help you make the right decisions at critical times.

There's one thing that isn't explained as fully in the book as I wish it could be. That is the precise relationship between the total head trauma (concussions and also subconcussive blows) that a child absorbs playing football and hockey and, to a lesser degree, soccer and basketball and the possibility of developing a degenerative brain disease such as CTE as an adult. We don't know yet. The research continues, and it is possible that we will have the answer to that critical question soon, perhaps within a decade.

Until then, let's stick with what we do know. Repeat after me: No head trauma is good head trauma.

Acknowledgments

From our first days working on this book, we hoped athletes and their parents would help us tell the story of the head trauma crisis. With assistance from many of Dr. Cantu's patients, we reached that goal. Our deepest thanks go to Kayla and Kathy DiBiasie, Matt Glass, Dylan and Donna Mello, Kathy and Mary Kate Gallagher, Ann-Marie and Rose-Marie Fuchs, Alyssa Blood, James Orrigo, Joel Weiss, Chris Vanesian, Ellen Spacek, Mirela and Sheree Caron, Kristen Chapman, and Taylor Twellman.

Many others also offered support and encouragement throughout this project. We especially thank Chris Nowinski, Ann McKee and Bob Stern, co-directors at the Center for the Study of Traumatic Encephalopathy at Boston University. Thanks also to Sharon Hoover, Tom Brady Sr., Patrice Bergeron, Kent Hughes, John Gagliardi, Sylvia Mackey, T.J. Cooney, Dan Lopez, and Ridge Diven. Special thanks go to Alan Schwarz, who introduced us and suggested this partnership.

Our literary agents, Meg Thompson and Andrew Blauner, offered encouragement and guidance at just the right moments, especially in the early days of the project.

At Houghton Mifflin Harcourt, the editorial assistant Ashley Gilliam was unfailingly helpful. Susan Canavan, our editor, was our greatest ally of all. Susan helped us see the project through the eyes of a committed and concerned sports parent, in part because she is one.

Dr. Robert Cantu and Mark Hyman

Appendix A

Today's Concussion Signs and Symptoms Checklist

Today's Date Date of Concussion	None (0)	Mild (1)	Moderate (2)	Severe (3)
Balance Issues		✓		
Confusion		✓		
Difficulty Concentrating			✓	
Difficulty Remembering			✓	
Dizziness				
Don't Feel Right/ Dinged/ Bell Rung				
Drowsy				
Fatigue/Low Energy				

Feeling in a Fog				
Feeling More Emotional				
Feeling Slowed Down				
Headache/Head Pressure				
Irritability				
Loss of Consciousness	No LOC	< 30 sec	1 min – 5 min	> 5 min
Nausea/Vomiting				
Neck Pain				
Nervous/Anxious				
Numbness/ Tingling				
Ringing in the Ears				
Sadness				
Sensitivity to Light				
Sensitivity to Noise				
Sleeping Less Than Usual				
Sleeping More Than Usual				
Trouble Falling Asleep				
Visual Problems/ Blurred Vision				

Athletes should score themselves on the above symptoms based on how they feel today (i.e., 0 = not present, 1 = mild, 2 = moderate, 3 = severe).

Symptom Load _4_ /26   Symptom Score _6_ (Max. 78, 26 × 3)   Concussion Grade ____

Note: Concussion grades are referenced on page 13 and in Appendix D.

Symptom load equals total number of symptoms
Symptom score equals sum of individual symptom scores

Appendix B

Cumulative Concussion Signs and Symptoms Checklist

Note: See page 9 for instructions on how to fill out form.

Today's Date Date of Concussion	None (0)	Mild (1)	Moderate (2)	Severe (3)
Balance Issues			1-2	
Confusion		2-1		
Difficulty Concentrating				
Difficulty Remembering				
Dizziness				
Don't Feel Right/ Dinged/ Bell Rung				
Drowsy				
Fatigue/Low Energy				

Feeling in a Fog				
Feeling More Emotional				
Feeling Slowed Down				
Headache/Head Pressure				
Irritability				
Loss of Consciousness	No LOC	< 30 sec	1 min – 5 min	> 5 min
Nausea/Vomiting				
Neck Pain				
Nervous/Anxious				
Numbness/ Tingling				
Ringing in the Ears				
Sadness				
Sensitivity to Light				
Sensitivity to Noise				
Sleeping Less Than Usual				
Sleeping More Than Usual				
Trouble Falling Asleep				
Visual Problems/ Blurred Vision				

Number of concussions you have had ___ Dates of concussions _____

How did/do you feel? Athletes should score themselves on the above symptoms based on how they felt at the time of each concussion and today (i.e., 0 = not present, 1 = mild, 2 = moderate, 3 = severe).

Symptom Load ___ /26   Symptom Score ___ (Max. 78, 26 × 3)   Concussion Grade ___

Appendix C

Concussion Patient History Intake Form

Patient Name: _____
Date: _____
Position Played: _____
Team: _____

CONCUSSION HISTORY:

		Y	N
	Have you ever been diagnosed with a concussion or had your "bell rung" or had symptoms in the check-off list you completed after a hit?		
	Have you ever lost consciousness as a result of a head injury? HOW LONG: _____		
	Have you ever been hospitalized as a result of a head injury? WHERE: _____ DETAILS: _____		
	Have you ever had any imaging studies done of your brain? (CT, MRI, DTI, other?) NAME:_____ DETAILS: _____		
	Date of most recent concussion		
	Date of most recent imaging studies		
	ADDITIONAL RISK FACTORS: PERSONAL HISTORY		
	Migraine Headaches		
	ADD/ADHD		
	Dyslexia		
	Other Learning Disabilities		
	Depression		
	Anxiety		
	Panic Attacks		
	Other Psychiatric Disorders		
	Seizure Disorder		
	Are you on any medications? If so, list: _____ _____ _____ _____ _____		

LIST FAMILY MEMBER	FAMILY HISTORY:		
	Migraine Headaches		
	ADD/ADHD		
	Dyslexia		
	Other Learning Disabilities		
	Depression		
	Anxiety		
	Panic Attacks		
	Other Psychiatric Disorders		
	Seizure Disorder		

Appendix D

*Guidelines for Return to Play
After Concussion(s) That Season*

	First Concussion	Second Concussion	Third Concussion
Grade 1 - Mild	May return to play if asymptomatic* for one week.	Return to play in two weeks if asymptomatic at that time for one week.	Terminate season; may return to play next season if asymptomatic.
Grade 2 - Moderate	Return to play after asymptomatic for one week.	Minimum of one month; may return to play then if asymptomatic for one week; consider terminating season.	Terminate season; may return to play next season if asymptomatic.
Grade 3 - Severe	Minimum of one month; may then return to play if asymptomatic for one week.	Terminate season; may return to play next season if asymptomatic.	

* No headache, dizziness, or impaired orientation, concentration, or memory during rest or exertion

Index

Page numbers in italics refer to photographs and illustrations.